HOW MUCH FOR A LEG?

Assessing the process of assessment of non-pecuniary personal injury damages in Scotland

WILLIAM J STEWART

DUNDEE UNIVERSITY PRESS
2010

First published in Great Britain in 2010 by
Dundee University Press
University of Dundee
Dundee DD1 4HN

www.dup.dundee.ac.uk

Copyright © William J Stewart

ISBN 978 1 84586 093 6

All rights reserved. No part of this publication may be reproduced, stored, or transmitted in any form, or by any means electronic, mechanical or photocopying, recording or otherwise, without the express written permission of the publisher.

The right of William J Stewart to be identified as the author of this work has been asserted in accordance with the Copyright, Designs and Patents Act 1988.

No natural forests were destroyed to make this product; only farmed timber was used and replanted.

British Library Cataloguing-in-Publication Data
A catalogue record for this book is available on request from the British Library

Typeset by Waverley Typesetters, Warham
Printed and bound by Bell & Bain Ltd, Glasgow

HOW MUCH FOR A LEG?

FOR
THE SCHOOL OF LAW,
UNIVERSITY OF STIRLING

CONTENTS

Preface vii
Table of Cases ix
Table of Legislation xiii

1. Introduction 1
2. Alternative Methods of Assessment 19
3. Analysis and Assessment of the Assessment Process 29
4. Conclusions 49

Appendices

    Appendix 1: Court-Disputed Non-Pecuniary Loss (Low Value) 63

    Appendix 2: Court-Disputed Non-Pecuniary Damages (Medium Value) (JSB Use) (Other Disputed Issues) 69

    Appendix 3: How Much for a Leg? 73

    Appendix 4: A Reconstruction of the CICA 2001 Tariff of Selected Listed Injuries (Allocated up to £4,400 by Value Rather Than by Injury) 84

    Appendix 5: What People Say the Damages Should Be 91

Bibliography 93
Index 97

PREFACE

When confronted with the question "How much for a leg?", members of the public who are not standing in a fast-food chicken bar may, depending on their age, immediately think of huge insured sums for the limbs of Mae West in the past or David Beckham in the present. However, these sums reflect the earning capacity of these famous body parts. This book is not about that: rather, it is about the pain and suffering that any person would experience if their said limb was seriously injured. Of course, it is not just about legs and considers how awards for a whole range of injuries are arrived at in Scotland and how it might be done better.

I am grateful to Professor Fraser Davidson and Dr Kay Goodall for support during the project (although they have no responsibility for the text). Thanks too to Alison, who was spared research duties this time but who read the text. Thanks to the publishers' reader. Finally, thanks to Dr Carole Dalgleish for seeing the work through to its conclusion.

BILL STEWART
The Law School
Airthrey Castle
University of Stirling
October 2009

TABLE OF CASES

	Page
Admiralty Commrs *v* SS Valeria [1922] 2 AC 242	29
Agnew *v* Scott Lithgow, IH, 1 April 2003; OH, 5 April 2002	59
Allan *v* Scott [1972] SC 59; 1972 SLT 45	50
Andrews *v* Hill, unreported, Romford County Court, 21 May 2004	67
Armstrong *v* Brake Brothers (Frozen Foods) Ltd 2003 SLT (Sh Ct) 58	16, 66, 68
Baigent *v* British Broadcasting Corporation 2001 SC 281; 2001 SLT 427	7, 16
Barker *v* Murdoch 1977 SLT (Notes) 75	83
Blackhall *v* MacInnes 1997 SLT 649	83
Burke *v* Glasgow City Council [2005] CSOH 155	59
Callaghan *v* Southern General Hospital NHS Trust 2000 SLT 1058	16
Carling *v* W P Bruce 2007 SLT 743	17
Casey *v* Cartwright [2006] EWCA Civ 1280; [2007] 2 All ER 78	37
Chambers *v* Forbes, unreported, Sh Miller, Ayr Sh Ct, 12 August 2005	68
Clarke *v* McFadyen 1990 SLT 277	83
Conway *v* Hytec Hydraulic Engineering Ltd, unreported, Sh Bicket, Hamilton, 23 March 2007	59
D (a child) *v* Bernard Shenton Ltd, Current Law Cases (2003) 1 QR 15	67, 68
D's Parent and Guardian *v* Argyll and Clyde Acute Hospitals NHS Trust 2003 SLT 511	16
Dall *v* Gaughan 2004 SCLR 1073	71
Deans *v* George Newberry Coachbuilders, unreported, Airdrie Sh Ct, 13 September 2005	59
Dickson *v* Hastings (No 1) 2007 SLT (Sh Ct) 161	16
Dickson *v* Hastings (No 2) 2007 SLT (Sh Ct) 164	17
Downie *v* Chief Constable, Strathclyde Police 1998 SLT 8	16
Duncanson *v* South Ayrshire Council 1999 SLT 519	16, 17
Duthie *v* Macfish Ltd 2001 SLT 833	16, 50
Elliot *v* Glasgow Corporation 1922 SC 146	39
Emslie *v* Bell, unreported, Lord Menzies, 12 August 2004	72
Fairley *v* Thomson, unreported, Sh Allan, Edinburgh Sh Ct, 2 September 2004	68
Ferguson *v* City Refrigeration Holdings (UK) Ltd 2005 Rep LR 117	68, 69
Fubri *v* Jones, CA No 199, 30 March 1979	8
Gallacher *v* Lanarkshire Health Board 1999 SLT 166	16
Girvan *v* Inverness Farmers Dairy 1998 SC (HL) 1; 1995 SLT 735	10, 11, 16, 30, 52

Girvan v Inverness Farmers Dairy (No 2) 1998 SLT 21; 1996 SLT 63 16
Graham v Marshall Food Group Ltd 1998 SLT 1448 16
Grassie v MacLaren 2000 SLT 944 16

Haddow v Glasgow City Council 2005 SLT 1219 16
Hamilton v Fife Health Board 1993 SC 369; 1993 SLT 624 5
Hawkes v Wynn 2002 SLT 1227 16
Heasman v J M Taylor & Partners 2002 SC 326; 2002 SLT 451 .... 11, 34
Heil v Rankin [2000] 2 WLR 1173 50

J v Fife Council 2007 SLT 85 .... 17, 50
— v — 2009 SLT 160 24

Kearsley v Klarfeld [2005] EWCA Civ 1510; [2006] 2 All ER 303 37
Kelly v Glasgow Corporation 1951 SC (HL) 15 39
Kerr v Newalls Insulation Co Ltd 1997 SLT 723 16
King v Bristow Helicopters [2002] UKHL 7; 2002 SC (HL) 59; 2002 SLT 378 5
Kumar v Kumar, 1997 Kemp and Kemp F5-014 71

Lamont v Cameron's Exrx 1997 SLT 1147 .... 16, 77
Leebody v Liddle 2000 SCLR 495 71
Lewis v Richardson 2002 SLT 272 16
Lightbody v Upper Clyde Shipbuilders Ltd 1998 SLT 884 .... 16, 17

MacAngus v Harry Lawson Ltd 1981 SLT (Notes) 94 83
McCallum v Paterson 1969 SC 85 39
McDyer v Celtic Football and Athletic Co Ltd (No 2) 2001 SLT 1387 .... 14, 16, 17
Macey-Lillie v Lanarkshire Health Board 2001 SLT 215 16
McKenna v British Railways Board 2003 SLT 1300 16
McKenzie v Barclay Curle Ltd 2002 SLT 649 16
McKenzie v Cape Building Products Ltd 1995 SLT 695 16
Mackenzie v Digby Brown & Co 1992 SLT 891 5
Mackenzie v H D Fraser & Sons 2001 SLT 116 16
McKeown v Lord Advocate 2002 SLT 269 16
MacKintosh v Morrice's Exrs 2007 SC 6; 2006 SLT 853 6
MacLean v Lothian and Borders Fire Brigade 1999 SLT 702 .... 15, 16
McManus v British Railways Board 1993 SC 557 9
Manson v Skinner 2000 SLT (Sh Ct) 161 .... 12, 16
Monaghan v Sim, unreported, Sh Baird, Glasgow Sh Ct, 29 September 2005 67
Morris v Sutherland, unreported, Sh Dunbar, Dunfermline Sh Ct, 3 August 2006 67
Morrison v Barton 1994 SLT 653 83
Mulroy v Garland, Butterworths Quantum No 970 71
Munnoch v Tay-Forth Foundries Ltd [2007] CSOH 159 70

Penny v J Ray McDermott Diving International Inc 2004 SLT 253 16
Power v Kitchener, Kemp and Kemp, para C2–037 83
Prentice v William Thyne Ltd 1989 SLT 336 83
Pugh v Scott 2002 Rep LR 112 .... 66, 69
Purves v Joydisc Ltd 2003 SLT (Sh Ct) 64 16

Quinn v Bowie 1987 SLT 575 67

R v Secretary of State for the Home Department [1995] 2 WLR 464 20
Rees v Darlington Memorial Hospital NHS Trust [2004] 1 AC 309 .... 21, 30
Robson v Glasgow City Council 2003 SLT 788 16
Ross v Harper 2004 SLT 353 16

Scully v Hoogstraten, 1993, Butterworths Quantum No 948 71
Shaher v British Aerospace Flying College Ltd 2003 SC 540 .... 10, 39
Smith v Shaw & McInnes Ltd, unreported, OH, Lord McEwan, 24 April 2001 59
Stanners v Graham Builders Merchants Ltd 1995 SLT 728 16
Stirling v Norwest Holst Ltd (No 2) 1998 SLT 1359 16
Symington v Milne, unreported, Edinburgh Sh Ct, 4 May 2007 63

Taggart v Shell (UK) Ltd 1996 SLT 795 16
Tudhope v Finlay Park t/a Park Hutchison Solicitors 2004 SLT 783 5

Wallace v Paterson 2002 SLT 563 16
White and Carter (Councils) Ltd v McGregor 1962 SC (HL) 1 6

Young v Scottish Coal (Deep Mining) Co Ltd 2002 SLT 1215 16

ECtHR
Hatton v UK, Chamber 2, October 2001; Grand Chamber, 8 July 2003 33
Maurice v France 11810/03, 6 October 2005 .... 32, 33
Öneryildiz v Turkey, Chamber Judgment, 18 June 2002; Grand Chamber,
30 November 2004 .... 32, 33

Germany
Decision BGH, 6 July 1955 49

Netherlands
Baardman v Ns, Amsterdam Court of Appeal, 12 August 2004, LJN AR2333 33

TABLE OF LEGISLATION

Page

Eire

2003	Personal Injuries Assessment Board Act	21
	s 3(a)	21
	(b)	21
	(c)	21
	(d)	22
	s 14	22
	s 17	23
	s 54(1)(b)	22
2007	Personal Injuries Assessment Board (Amendment) Act	21

European Union

1950	European Convention on Human Rights	34
	Protocol 1, Art 1	32, 33
	Art 8	33
	Art 13	33

Scotland

2006	Family Law (Scotland) Act	6

United Kingdom

1973	Prescription and Limitation (Scotland) Act	5
	s 22(1)	5
1976	Damages (Scotland) Act	6
	s 1(4)	7
1992	Social Security Contributions and Benefits Act	58
1993	Damages (Scotland) Act	6
	s 1(1)	7
1995	Private International Law (Miscellaneous Provisions) Act	5
	s 11(3)	5
2006	Compensation Act	40

1. INTRODUCTION

PRELIMINARY

"How much for my leg?" This is an apparently simple question which might be asked of a lawyer by a citizen who has sustained a wrongful injury to the said limb. But, in Scotland, no fixed answer can be given. Nor can any official range of possible figures be given. Only after some serious professional work, perhaps taking many hours, can a range of figures be suggested. It need not be like this.

Every so often it may be instructive to review and analyse apparently routine aspects of the legal system, known to some or all of the members of a profession concerned in what is a specialism, to ascertain whether and to what extent what is done is desirable or, more broadly, and to use a phrase currently in vogue, "fit for purpose". This study sets out what is done legally and practically in relation to the assessment of non-pecuniary personal injury damages. It compares and contrasts the position in Scotland with other systems. Criticism and discussion based on this analysis are offered and proposals for improvement are canvassed. The present system has grown up almost entirely as a tradition of the legal profession. Yet it is largely the tax-paying, premium-paying public who meet the costs and have little or no say in what these costs should be. Nor what the awards might be. This contrasts with, say, the tax and social security systems which are in the political arena. Among the most substantial transaction costs involved are those incurred to the legal process, although it must be appreciated that much of that money may well be disbursed to courts and to medical and other witnesses. This is not to say that there is any conspiracy among the legal profession to maintain an inefficient, unfair and costly system: just that it is difficult for any commercial person to justify devoting time to devising systems that deprive their business of income! A leading academic has said, on the issue of improving the law of damages in general (of which this study is a small subset):

> "The main difficulty is that the subject is far too important to be entrusted solely to lawyers, but nobody else understands it well enough to be able

to propose the deep-rooted reforms really required. The one body which might have been able to do this job – the [English] Law Commission – is far too closely wedded to the system and its underlying value structure to be able to bring to bear the independent scrutiny the system needs. In the long run the only solution to the difficulty must lie in educating the public to understand more fully the nature of the system we live under, and who pays its costs. Perhaps lawyers too need educating, because though they may understand the nuts and bolts of the system, they do not see it in full perspective."[1]

The subject being considered in this study is smaller than the whole system of damages. Nor is it directed at the so-called "compensation culture".[2] This study is neutral in that regard – if cost is to be saved it is for others to say whether it might go to lower general taxation and lower premiums or simply leave more money in government coffers and the household accounts. Alternatively, if cost is saved, more could be paid to victims or new victims found.[3]

So it is hoped that this study inspires those outside the profession to ask whether it might not be desirable to improve the present system and that one or more of the options presented might be thought worthy. On a final note, the remarks of Atiyah above related to the English Law Commission. The Scottish Law Commission is the source of most of the systemic rational law reform in Scotland. Since devolution it has been asked to do more and has done more. It would *not* be right to assume that *our* Commission is far too closely wedded to lawyers' systems. After all, it was the Scottish Law Commission and the Scottish Parliament that actually abolished the feudal system in which all living lawyers had been trained and were experienced. As is noted below, on a closely related topic the Scottish Law Commission at least included the issue of a tariff in a recent discussion paper,[4] albeit declining to follow it through after consultation.[5]

The only problem with hoping for something from the Commission is that it appears to be very busy indeed. It attends to its own programmes.

---

[1] P S Atiyah, *The Damages Lottery* (1997), p 173.
[2] See, eg, E Lee, J Peysner *et al*, *Compensation Crazy: Do we blame and claim too much?* (Institute of Ideas, 2002; K Williams, "Britain's 'Compensation Culture' Reviewed" (2005) 25 LS 499.
[3] Not, of course, an option favoured by Atiyah.
[4] Scottish Law Commission, *Damages for Wrongful Death* (SLC DP No 135, 2007) (henceforth "SLC, *Wrongful Death*"), paras 3.56–3.66. A few passages in this book were included in the author's response to that discussion paper. This book does *not* seek to re-open that debate on fatal damages.
[5] Scottish Law Commission, *Report on Damages for Wrongful Death* (SLC No 213, 2008) (henceforth "SLC Report"), paras 3.51–3.52.

It co-operates with the (English) Law Commission in relation to reform of common UK laws. It must now respond to ever-increasing and no doubt justified referrals from the devolved Scottish Government. It would probably need some socio–political–economic pressure in order to engage Scottish Law Commission activity. And it must be recalled that while the Scottish Law Commission is expert indeed in the law, it relies on such outside help as it can afford on other topics and the happenstance of whether and to what extent it receives helpful responses. Major reform in this area is more likely to require substantial preliminary inter-disciplinary work. Equally unsatisfactory of course would be any knee-jerk political solution designed simply to save money. While the Scottish Law Commission would be aware that the (English) Law Commission rejected substantial reform in its 1999 report, and would of course benefit from that work, it would not be at all bound by that outcome.[6] It may be that, now, in Scotland, the Scottish people and Parliament might, like the majority (60 per cent) of consultees to the English report,[7] prefer to see levels of damages being set centrally by some form of Compensation Advisory Board. Similarly, the rejection of a tariff by 74 per cent of consultees to the (English) Commission may have been overly influenced by the then current disquiet over the criminal injuries compensation tariff, which has since abated. The English Law Commission arranged to discover what the public thought awards should be[8] and there is some discussion of this below.

It should not be thought that there is any complacency in Scotland about the overall civil justice system. There have already been dramatic reforms to court procedures by the court itself,[9] expedited informal protocols agreed between the solicitors' branch and insurers,[10] and not least a full Review of civil justice chaired by the Lord Justice-Clerk (Lord

---

[6] *Damages for Personal Injury: Non-pecuniary Loss* (Law Com No 257, 1999) (henceforth "Law Com Damages").
[7] *Ibid*, para 3.120.
[8] *Ibid*, Appendix B: "Research Carried Out by the Office for National Statistics Into Public Perceptions of What Damages for Non-pecuniary Loss in Personal Injury Cases Should Be" (henceforth "ONS"). This included data obtained from Scotland: see ONS, pp 140 and 145 (see extract in Appendix 5).
[9] G Garrett, "New Deal for PI Claims" (2005) (Dec) JLSS 28; G Garrett, "A Breach of Protocol" 2008 (Feb) JLSS 14.
[10] For the history and operation of the reforms, see E Samuels, *Managing Procedure: Evaluation of New Rules for actions of damages for, or arising from, personal injuries in the Court of Session (Chapter 43) – Research Findings* (Scottish Parliament, Social Research, Civil Justice, Research Findings 1/2007).

Gill) whose report was published in September of 2009.[11] This study on a narrow topic is not a response to that magnum opus.[12] Rather, it is hoped that the core argument of this study might inform a little of the debate that is likely to follow upon reception of the Gill Report which has now been handed back to the Scottish Ministers. Accordingly, indications appear where the arguments in this study are in harmony with the major recommendations and philosophy of the Gill Report. It should be said that the fact that the Gill Report has not made any recommendations along the lines of the ideas this study ought not to be held against these ideas. The Gill Review was admittedly not comprehensive and was intentionally a limited exercise – although an extensive and impressive one – trying to propose pragmatic reforms that could be readily implemented at reasonable cost.[13] While in places this book proposes complete and fundamental reform, more modest limited alternatives are suggested herein, which, it is submitted, fit the philosophy and some of the detail of the Gill Report.

So while this is entirely a legal study, engaging theory and practice, it seeks to convince a wider audience as well. To this end, Appendices 1–3 are included, showing in print some of the "nuts and bolts" to which Atiyah refers, known only to lawyers, to give flesh to the arguments in the study for the benefit of the lay reader. These have been selected and lightly edited. Appendices 1–3, which comprise extracts from court decisions, have been picked to make the point but also because they are both typical and excellent of their type.

Finally, there is much interest around Europe in comparative personal injury law[14] and Scotland has not merited consideration in all of these

---

[11] *Report of the Scottish Civil Courts Review*, Scottish Civil Courts Review, Chair Lord Gill, September 2009 (henceforth "Gill Report"). This is, at the time of writing, available online. Chapter 3 is a short guide to the civil courts in Scotland, written for the lay person, and is commended to lay readers of this text: http://www.scotcourts.gov.uk/civilcourtsreview/ (accessed 8/10/09).

[12] Having been researched and written before the Gill Report was published.

[13] Gill Report, vol 1, p ii.

[14] W V H Rogers (ed), *Damages for Non-Pecuniary Loss in a Comparative Perspective* (2001) (henceforth "Rogers, *Comparative Perspective*"); M Bona and P Mead (eds), *Personal Injury Compensation in Europe* (2003) (henceforth "Bona & Mead, *PICE*"); D McIntosh and M Holmes (eds), *Personal Injury Awards in EU and EFTA Countries* (3rd edn, 2003) (henceforth "McIntosh & Holmes"); B Markesinis *et al*, *Compensation for Personal Injury in English, German and Italian Law: A Comparative Outline* (2005) (henceforth "Markesinis, *Compensation*"); European Group of Tort Law, *Principles of European Tort Law: Text and Commentary* (2005) (this latter incorporates the earlier workings comprised in Rogers, *Comparative Perspective*).

exercises[15] and so it is hoped that this volume will be of value to such comparative lawyers in future.

PERSONAL INJURY

The phrase "personal injury" has been the object of much debate in many different contexts. The broken leg of the injured workman may be a paradigm, at least in practice.[16] The apparent simplicity of the phrase is misleading. Difficulties have arisen with cases such as the professional neglect in pursuing a prior case for injury to a person;[17] nervous shock;[18] and ante-natal injury.[19]

Criminal injuries compensation, discussed in general terms below, has a specific and quite wide definition of its own.[20] It is not entirely clear whether or not death can properly be called a personal injury. It may be the very worst type or alternatively it may define the limit of personal injury. Conduct which would have caused personal injury had the victim not lived may be called "fatal injury". In Scots law the damages payable on wrongful death are now the subject of what is effectively a partial code and one which has been thoughtfully amended from time to time for juridical

---

[15] There is an explicit full treatment by A S Logan in Bona & Mead, *PICE*. The 3rd edn of McIntosh & Holmes includes a section on Scotland by A H Lockhart, A K Brown and F Thomson.

[16] The Twelve Tables of the Roman Law (circa 450 BC) provided fixed penalties as well as an incentive to negotiate: "Table 8:2. If a person has maimed another's limb, let there be retaliation in kind unless he makes agreement for composition with him. 3. If he has broken or bruised freeman's bone with hand or club, he shall undergo penalty of 300 pieces; if slave's, 150. 4. If he has done simple harm [to another], penalties shall be 25 pieces" (A Watson, "Personal Injuries in the XII Tables" (1975) 43 *Tijdschrift voor Rechtsgeschiedenis* 213, quoting the translation by E H Warmington in his n 2).

[17] *Mackenzie* v *Digby Brown & Co* 1992 SLT 891, considering the now superseded Rules of Court 1965, r 89A(1); *Tudhope* v *Finlay Park t/a Park Hutchison Solicitors* 2004 SLT 783, considering r 43.1(1). For the opposite view, see an earlier hearing in the same case at 2003 SLT 1305!

[18] *King* v *Bristow Helicopters* [2002] UKHL 7; 2002 SC (HL) 59; 2002 SLT 378 (bodily injury does not include mental harm). The Prescription and Limitation (Scotland) Act 1973 specially extends the meaning of "personal injury" to include disease or any impairment of physical or mental condition: s 22(1). The Private International Law (Miscellaneous Provisions) Act 1995 includes disease or any impairment of physical or mental condition: s 11(3).

[19] *Hamilton* v *Fife Health Board* 1993 SC 369; 1993 SLT 624.

[20] "Personal injury" includes physical injury (including fatal injury), mental injury (that is temporary mental anxiety, medically verified, or a disabling mental illness confirmed by psychiatric diagnosis) and disease (that is a medically recognised illness or condition): Criminal Injuries Compensation Scheme 2008, para 9.

and political reasons,[21] and a code which indeed came under review again while this research was under way.[22] Thus, in this legal context personal injury is everything short of death.[23] The two issues are different *at least* for historical reasons.[24] Because of that, and the involvement of the Scottish Law Commission on the assessment of fatal claims,[25] fatal claims are not *directly* considered here. It will be seen throughout that there may be good grounds for considering some issues arising in fatal claims where there are similarities in the assessment process (albeit the legal and historical background is different).

NON-PECUNIARY DAMAGES

We are not concerned with contract debt. While it may be said that if you do not pay the £10,000 you promised to pay, I am suing for damages, the amount is more properly categorised as a debt.[26] Liquidate damages which are contractually specified may indeed be "damages" but, by definition, they do not require assessment.

So the damages with which we are concerned are unliquidated damages. In Scots law, unliquidated damages may be sought when the workman's leg is injured arising out of either delict or breach of an implied term of the contract of employment to take care. This is not necessarily the case in other systems. Traditionally, the damages are divided between patrimonial loss and solatium.[27] Unfortunately, neither term is free from controversy. Fortunately, for the purpose of this volume, the core type

---

[21] Principally the Damages (Scotland) Act 1976 and the Damages (Scotland) Act 1993, as amended by various legislative enactments critical in detail, such as the Family Law (Scotland) Act 2006.
[22] SLC, *Wrongful Death* and SLC Report.
[23] Recently confirmed in the opinion of the court delivered by Lord MacLean in *MacKintosh v Morrice's Exrs* 2007 SC 6 at 10; 2006 SLT 853 at 855: "This is a case concerned with deaths which occurred directly and immediately as a result of admitted negligent driving. There is no claim for damages in respect of personal injuries. Neither deceased had in their lifetime a right to damages vested in them in respect of personal injuries. Neither suffered any patrimonial loss in their lifetime as a result of the accident. Where death results from a negligent act, as in this case, relatives or dependants, such as the pursuers, are entitled to claim for loss of society (solatium) and, where it is justified factually, for loss of support."
[24] The history and development are set out in Part 2 of SLC, *Wrongful Death*.
[25] See SLC, *Wrongful Death*, paras 3.63–3.65 in particular.
[26] *White and Carter (Councils) Ltd* v *McGregor* 1962 SC (HL) 1.
[27] "Solatium" is a term of art in Spain: M Martín-Casals, J Ribot and J Solé in Rogers, *Comparative Perspective* at pp 197–198.

of solatium – unliquidated damages for non-financial loss – is the focus of the inquiry. Solatium describes, among other things, the pain and suffering damages awarded when the leg of the workman is wrongfully broken. Other systems have different heads (or categories) of damages claim within non-pecuniary loss which are sometimes treated in different ways. In Scots law, defamation is seen as delictual and produces damages which include the financial losses of reputation but, taking account perhaps of an *actio iniuriarum* civilian heritage, will allow damages for the affront where there is no damage to financial reputation. These non-pecuniary losses, albeit termed "solatium", are not treated in the same way as personal injury damages.[28] In the case of fatal injuries, statutory terms are in play, replacing the use of solatium in this particular context.[29] The concern of this volume is payments made for pain and suffering and not for lost earnings. This uncertainty of language use for categorisation of damages is not good for legal science yet in this particular area it is not at all uncommon, being found in English law,[30] with *Schmerzensgeld* in Germany,[31] and in the relatively new *danno biologico* of Italian law.[32] Belgian law has similar problems with four terms (*patrimonial* loss, *extra-patrimonial* loss, *moral* and *material* damage), with some confusion as to meaning.[33] Few terms are interchangeable, although there can be overlapping content.[34]

ASSESSMENT

Assessment in this context is to do with weighing up. It is, more narrowly, quantification, which answers the question "How much?". Thus, practitioners operate within an exercise of "quantification of damages". The task is to arrive at the proper "quantum" or amount.

---

[28] *Baigent* v *British Broadcasting Corporation* 2001 SC 281; 2001 SLT 427.
[29] Damages (Scotland) Act 1976, s 1(4), as amended by the Damages (Scotland) Act 1993, s 1(1). A new terminology is offered by the Scottish Law Commission, SLC Report, para 3.52.
[30] Markesinis, *Compensation*, p 2.
[31] *Ibid*, p 4. See also Decision BGH, 6 July 1955, translated by Y P Salmon, in W Van Gerven *et al*, *Cases, Materials and Text on National, Supranational and International Tort Law* (2000), p 754.
[32] Markesinis, *Compensation*, p 7.
[33] H Cousy and D Droshout in Rogers, *Comparative Perspective* at p 29.
[34] For an analysis of what does or does not fall within non-pecuniary loss across Europe, albeit not including Scotland, see W V H Rogers, "Comparative Report of a project Carried Out by the European Centre for Tort and Insurance Law" in Rogers, *Comparative Perspective* (SpringerWein, New York, 2001).

Assessment is not to do with liability. Of course, scholars have known for a very long time that what may look like working out the amount of damages (mensuration) may in fact be a hidden aspect of liability.[35] Assessment proceeds upon a prior exercise of determining the heads (or categories) of damage. It is difficult to measure something before it is identified. The position in Scotland is identical to that in England: "There is no mathematical or scientific calculation involved in arriving at the appropriate figure."[36]

The Scottish Law Commission said: "It must always be remembered that the quantification of the losses sustained by a victim of personal injuries is an issue of fact. While particular conventions have developed to aid the assessment of the victim's losses, these are technically not rules of law although some at least appear to be treated as such."[37] This is a fair summary of the position but understates the way in which previous decisions are in fact used as if they were authorities – this can be seen in Appendices 1–3. The appearance of efficacy of previous cases as rules of law is encouraged by the fact that decisions may be appealed and are often appealed. Usually there is no appeal on a point of fact and exceptional cases are rare indeed.

THE TIME OF ASSESSMENT

(1) Damages are usually assessed authoritatively at the end of a case.[38]
(2) Sometimes they may be assessed during a case.[39]
(3) A raised case may settle on the basis of a compromise between the assessment of parties.
(4) The case may settle prior to litigation on correspondence on the basis of a compromise.
(5) To be complete, it might be worth saying that some claims might not be assessed at all, as where an insurer or a regular wrongdoer

---

[35] G Gilmore, *Death of Contract* (1974), Chapter 2, "Development".
[36] Markesinis, *Compensation*, p 50, citing *Fuhri* v *Jones*, CA No 199, 30 March 1979.
[37] SLC, *Wrongful Death*, para 2.6.
[38] When is the end of a case? That varies, as discussed below under the rubric "By whom are damages assessed?".
[39] As where a sheriff court case is sent to a proof split between quantum and liability in which case it is possible for quantum to be determined first: Ordinary Cause Rules, r 29(6). See generally T Welch (ed), *Macphail's Sheriff Court Practice* (3rd edn, 2006), para 8.61.

simply issues instructions to pay claims beneath a certain amount, preferring this cost of settlement to the transactional costs of litigation.

ASSESSORS

Damages are assessed authoritatively by judges.[40] Usually the first (and possibly final) decision is taken by a sheriff in the sheriff court or by a Lord Ordinary in the Outer House of the Court of Session. It is usually a first-instance exercise. It may, subject to restrictive rules,[41] be carried out of new (afresh), by an appeal court such as the sheriff principal on appeal or by the Inner House or even by the Supreme Court of the United Kingdom.[42] In the unlikely case where the ground of appeal is that the lower court failed to assess damages at all, damages may be assessed by the appeal court should it so wish, this being the first assessment. Interestingly, where a judge decides that the pursuer has lost his case, the practice is that damages are still assessed. This is theoretically interesting because it provides a database of assessments with a data set greater than the number of awards of damages made. It is also interesting because it tends to suggest that the process of assessment is not usually going to be at all controversial. The most likely reason for doing this is that if there is an appeal by the pursuer in relation to the decision against the pursuer, time will be saved either by the appeal court not having to assess damages itself or precluding the need to have to remit the issue to the first-instance court.

Damages are assessed by the legal teams of parties with a view to reaching a compromise position. These legal teams may be at the highest level of Queen's Counsel to the lowest level of in-house specialist legal staff.

Damages may be assessed by persons who are neither lawyers nor parties, as in the case of unqualified claims handlers seeking to adjust with a clerk in an insurance company.[43]

---

[40] Here may be included other judicial figures and quasi-judicial figures or bodies seised of the same issue.
[41] To be overturned, an award for solatium must be such as can be described as "wholly unreasonable or clearly excessive": *McManus* v *British Railways Board* 1993 SC 557 per LJ-C Ross (delivering the opinion of the whole court) at 559.
[42] Formerly the Judicial Committee of the House of Lords.
[43] Practice in this regard is said to have changed in recent years. Traditionally, a case could be discussed with an experienced unqualified claims handler with a good knowledge of the system and, of course, access to the range of proper settlement figures. An experienced litigator has reported that "the insurers have moved to a call centre approach in which

Damages may be assessed by parties themselves. Knowledgeable parties may decide that they can assess some claims for themselves based on information they have collated themselves or which they obtain from the now more widely available legal sources such as the Internet. So, for example, damages may be assessed by a council official. Less knowledgeable pursuers, it must be said, often attempt the exercise themselves because of the frequent reports of enormous awards for minor injury recorded in the popular press. This phenomenon is not to be underestimated. The claimant has only this generalised information from the media and trust in any adviser on which to base any decision to settle.

In some cases damages may be assessed by a single non-judicial party, as where parties ask for the opinion of learned counsel.[44]

Damages may be assessed by lay jurors where there has been a jury trial, now much more common in Scotland, despite the institution being rare elsewhere. A very curious situation has arisen in relation to jury awards and is worth a detailed digression. Lay jurors are not at present allowed any guidance on how to come to their assessments.[45] As will be seen, courts avail themselves of at least some guidance on how cases have been assessed before – jurors are not given this information. There are arguments for and against that which are beyond the scope of this work. What has happened is that this "jury" data has been legally privileged by judicial decision. It has been accepted that sometimes judicial assessments become too low.[46] However, more dramatically, it was said, in a fatal case, that it is these jury awards that reflect society and give awards their essential legitimacy.[47] Even more interestingly, the Gill Review gave anxious consideration to whether or not jury trial should continue – and decided, on balance, that it should.[48] What is significant for this study is that the main reason given for keeping the jury trial is that it provides a calibrating figure for judicial awards.[49] This calibration is limited. A rule

---

such negotiations as there are tend to be conducted on the telephone with fairly junior personnel ... levels of knowledge among claims handlers range from the mediocre to woeful, particularly in employers' liability claims": G Garrett, "A Breach of Protocol" 2008 (Feb) JLSS 14 at 16.

[44] This is more suitable to a dispute between parties in an otherwise ongoing good faith relationship. In personal injuries cases it is more likely, if counsel's opinion is to be sought, that both sides obtain one of their own.

[45] *Girvan* v *Inverness Farmers Dairy* 1998 SC (HL) 1 at 20–22 per Lord Hope.

[46] *Shaher* v *British Aerospace Flying College Ltd* 2003 SC 540 at 542–543.

[47] *Ibid.*

[48] Gill Report, vol 1, vi–vii.

[49] *Ibid*, Chapter 4, paras 156–163.

of thumb operates to the effect that if the jury awards more than double what a judge would have awarded, the decision may be appealed.[50] So the jury *does not*, as a matter of law, get to set the levels. Indeed, it might be important that it does not, for, as the jury process is secret, it would place defenders in a difficult position in estimating settlements or in insuring their positions.[51] Jury awards will be taken into account by judges and in due course "jury" data would feed into the overall set of data. It is not officially collected. There is not all that much of it as jury cases, like others, do settle. So the position is reached where the true figure, is the jury figure. The jury does not know how to come to the figure, being given no relevant information. Its figure will be struck down if it is too high compared with previous awards about which it has no information and these previous figures are predominantly non-jury figures. This is logically defective. The anchoring figure – the judicial figure – is discussed below. If a better way of calibrating non-pecuniary awards could be found, there would be fewer reasons, if any, for retaining the civil jury trial. It might be noted that in pecuniary cases, with which we are concerned, the "more than double" rule does not apply to any significant error in calculating fixed pecuniary items – the jury has no special function here at all.

FINDING ASSESSMENTS

The location of any given assessment does not always map directly to a particular assessor.

Judicial opinions are the most transparent and authoritative sources. An ordinary decision is likely to reveal a consideration of two competing arguments and the selection of a position – usually preferring one or other or striking a position between the two. More rarely, a judge may carry out his own research and reach a position higher or lower than the maximum/minimum of the parties – although it would be usual to give parties the chance to comment on any such extra research. This is rare because the judicial function is traditionally to decide which of the two parties is correct and not to investigate. A decision on assessment alone is unlikely to appear in the law reports unless it raises a substantive point

---

[50] *Girvan* v *Inverness Farmers Dairy* 1998 SC (HL) 1 contains a full review of the history and development of this type of appeal and a statement of the present law on the matter of the highest authority.

[51] When jury trial was challenged by defenders as not being human rights compliant, the "rule of thumb" right of appeal helped defeat that challenge: *Heasman* v *J M Taylor & Partners* 2002 SC 326; 2002 SLT 451.

about heads of damage or a question of method. Sometimes, if a case is being reported in any event, the part dealing with assessment may be left in the report – or, as it may have nothing to do with a larger point of substantive law, might be left out. So as a source of information, reported cases have their limits.

Unreported cases are by definition not edited and will contain any discussion of assessment which the judge has decided to include. They are therefore both a full and an authoritative source. Jury verdicts which are unchallenged are a source of an assessment but the process by which the number is reached in a particular case is unknown to us.[52] It has been suggested that jury awards may be around twice the level of judicial assessments.[53]

Some actions are settled without even an unreported opinion and they may remain unknown save to those who collect them privately. There will be a court record. For reasons of practice and procedure, these are not entirely helpful. In cases where there is to be compensation recovery through the state welfare system, it is possible that the final court order will reflect a joint minute between the parties, allocating damages to various heads. In some cases an omnibus record may be found. In others there may simply be a record that the defender has been absolved from the claim (the money agreed having actually been paid).

Some claims do not even become actions and likewise may remain unknown.

There are other sources – not quite full reports.[54]

Available data is limited in Scotland. At one time only counsel had access to sufficient material – in opinions located in the Court of Session – to be able to say what a judge might do. With a small data set, prediction was naturally difficult. The bigger the data set and the better

---

[52] These are not formally reported but are noted in A Hajducki, QC, *Civil Jury Trials* (2nd edn, 2006) and from time to time in the *Reparation Law Reports*.

[53] See, eg, 2005 RepLR 90, in which the editor comments that his short review of a handful of cases indicates that jury awards were, roughly speaking, about twice that which a judge would have made.

[54] For example the "Quantum" notes in the *Reparation Law Reports* or notes in *Greens Weekly Digest*. These are regarded with some caution: "In that regard I should also add that I am somewhat wary of deriving too much assistance from case reports which are no more than brief digests. It seems to me that there must always be a risk with such digests that they do not convey the full picture which was before the court at the time. Nonetheless, as I have said, the cases referred to all appear to have involved more serious injuries than in the present case" (per Sh Pr C G B Nicholson, QC in *Manson v Skinner* 2000 SLT (Sh Ct) 161 at 164).

it is organised, the easier it is to predict. The development of the private publication *McEwan & Paton* provided a concise source which could be consulted, showing previous awards, reported and unreported. The data was organised to facilitate comparison. *Greens Weekly Digest* provided short notes available to the entire legal community outside Parliament House, with many unreported cases. Now, thanks to the Scottish Courts website, all relevant cases from the Court of Session appear (together with some others from the sheriff courts).

However, this recent expansion of available data may be slowing down. The editor of the *Reparation Law Reports* has noticed that there appear to be far fewer decisions from the Court of Session than there used to be and that accordingly it seems that the amount of guidance for the legal profession as to the appropriate levels of *solatium* for different injuries is reducing.[55]

JUDICIAL ASSESSMENT: THE PROCESS IN SCOTLAND

Following the model of adversarial procedure, the two sides interrogate the data located and examine the selected subset. This is then used to build arguments towards a particular sum or a range. Where the range of the pursuer's subset and the range of the defender's subset overlap or coincide, there is the possibility of settlement. If there is no overlap or coincidence then there is a lower possibility of settlement, worsening as the purser's bottom figure is distant from the defender's highest. Where no formal structures exist there will be a reluctance to exchange this data. The pursuer will not want to reveal "his" range in case he has undercalculated or in case he prevents the defender from overcalculating. The same approach may be taken by the defender. Defender reparation practice is more concentrated in fewer expert law firms and so the defender may be very keen to await an undervaluation from a less experienced pursuer's lawyer, although there are a good number of specialist pursuers' firms now.[56]

---

[55] D Kinloch, Editorial, *Greens Reparation Law Reports* 2006 (6) RepLR 123. Happily, the possible reason for this is the success of the new Court of Session rules in encouraging pre-proof meetings and exchanging valuations.

[56] This is the "one-shotter" versus the "repeat player" model. It is discussed in contemporary context in R Lewis, "Insurance and the tort system" (2005) 25 LS 85 at 89–90, citing the relevant earlier literature in his n 24. Lewis comments that "Claimant lawyers are now much more likely to be specialists and work in larger and much better organised firms than in the past. Relying upon Law Society figures, Goriely et al … note that even before April 2000 (when almost all legal aid was abolished for personal injury claims) solicitors

By the time the matter comes to a court, parties require to show their hand. This may be in a formal way, as where under the new Court of Session rules a schedule of damages must be served. Informally, in conjunction with that, or where the new rules do not apply, some indication will be given by rules requiring the listing of authorities (previous cases) which a party intends to put before the court in argument. This is consonant with the traditional view of litigation which sees the judge as deciding between opposing contentions rather than investigating matters for himself.[57] The settlement process out of court has been described as being in the shadow of the law: "legal claims are solved by the mutual prediction of a full court outcome. The proximity of the judicial process gives coercive power to negotiations, and establishes settlement norms with reference to decided cases. This is the daily stuff of our practitioner lives".[58]

This presentation of "authorities" is curious. A decision on the quantum of damages is not an authority in the sense that it can ever bind any court – even if there were (unusually) a decision of the Inner House fixing damages relevant to the case under consideration. This is because it is closely related to the facts of the individual cases. That said, reference to previous cases is very common. It is the method with which all in the process are familiar and this "precedent" approach has been adopted by default. One of the foundations of doctrines of precedent is the precept of justice that like cases be treated alike. Thus, reference to previous cases in the context of the assessment of damages may be thought to be better than nothing at all. Indeed, absent recent developments, it might be wondered how any consistent justice could be done otherwise.[59] It may still be the case that a situation can easily arise where without reference

---

were becoming increasingly specialised, and fewer firms were 'dabbling' in such work" (n 21). In Scotland, legal aid has *not* been abolished but strict quality control regimes, associated cost overheads and elements of fixed fees make it unlikely that there are very many occasional players.

[57] See, eg, *McDyer v Celtic Football and Athletic Co Ltd (No 2)* 2001 SLT 1387 per Lord McCluskey: "Each party presented a document entitled 'Schedule of damages' setting forth under 10 different heads the sums at which, in the submission of the author of the schedule, the court should assess the appropriate award. This way of presenting the matter has proved immensely helpful, especially when the parties took the opportunity to summarise in the body of the schedule their submissions, with reference to the evidence, and also noting relevant authorities" (at 1388).

[58] R Conway, "A Colossus in the room" 2008 (53) JLSS 14–16 at 15–16 (henceforth "Conway, *Colossus*").

[59] The Court of Session is based in Edinburgh and is collegiate including the appellate judges, and so there is every possibility of informal co-ordination. That said, the court is much larger than once it was.

to the meagre body of "authorities" there could be a serious divergence between "Sheriff Stingy" in the East and "Sheriff Bountiful" in the West.[60] Matters may improve considerably in this respect in future in that the Gill Report proposes a specialist personal injury court located in Edinburgh, with an all-Scotland jurisdiction.[61] People could still sue locally and would be allocated a specialist sheriff.

Perhaps typical of the modern approach to the use of previous cases is a *dictum* such as this:

> "As I have stated on a number of occasions, I do not generally find reference to authorities of much assistance when assessing solatium, which very much depends on the circumstances of a particular case. However I do find the analysis of Lord Eassie [in another case] helpful in the particular circumstances of this case, although I take the view that the overall injuries in that case were marginally worse than the present one."[62]

Interrogation of the data, at least in the first instance, is likely to be by way of *McEwan & Paton*.[63] This is entirely a privately written and privately published work carrying no official imprimatur.[64] Following tradition, *McEwan & Paton* is not always cited when used. Most likely it is used by counsel to locate the cases they wish to cite to the court and it is the case discovered in the book, rather than the book itself, which is cited. Aside from reporting the cases, perhaps the very most significant thing about the book is that the cases are organised on a "body parts" basis. It has been produced for utility and its longevity has demonstrated its success.

Quite a different path has, however, been taken in relation to assessment in recent times. It is the use made of the guidelines produced by the English Judicial Studies Board. Use of these guidelines in *Scotland* may have been enhanced by their inclusion in *McEwan & Paton*.[65] Despite the fierce independence of Scots law and the Scottish profession, these are increasingly being used in Scotland. So far as reported cases are

---

[60] Sheriffs are now linked by e-mail and it may be that a "virtual college" of sheriffs exists.
[61] Gill Report, Chapter 4, para 154.
[62] Lord Johnston in *MacLean* v *Lothian and Borders Fire Brigade* 1999 SLT 702 at 704.
[63] Or the newer competitor: S A Bennett, *Personal Injury Damages in Scotland* (2007, looseleaf).
[64] However, Robin McEwan became a judge as Lord McEwan; and Ann Paton is still a serving judge as Lady Paton and indeed sits in the Inner House.
[65] And they are in the newer S A Bennett, *Personal Injury Damages in Scotland* (2007, looseleaf).

concerned, they first appear in 1994.[66] This particular first appearance was in an unusual case as it was a motion to set aside a jury verdict as extravagant. At the time, jury trials had been revived after some period of desuetude. So the JSB may have been an attractive source in this 1994 case because the JSB took into account jury awards in England and was thus outside the logical loop. Being a decision of the Inner House (which later appeared in the House of Lords) it may have given practitioners confidence to cite this alien source in future. So quantitatively in the reports up to the end of 2007 there are three cases in 1995;[67] two cases in 1996;[68] two cases in 1997;[69] five cases in 1998;[70] three in 1999;[71] three in 2000;[72] five in 2001;[73] six in 2002;[74] five in 2003;[75] two in 2004;[76] one in 2005;[77] nil in 2006; and three in 2007.[78]

---

[66] *Girvan* v *Inverness Farmers Dairy* 1995 SLT 735. Note that cases cited in this section of the article are by way of data rather than authorities. Thus the SLT citations are used (rather than *Session Cases*) as it was from the SLT database that the cases were taken. Further, as with *Girvan*, any case cited in this section may have been appealed or reconsidered in another case.

[67] *Girvan* v *Inverness Farmers Dairy* 1995 SLT 735; *Stanners* v *Graham Builders Merchants Ltd* 1995 SLT 728; *McKenzie* v *Cape Building Products Ltd* 1995 SLT 695.

[68] *Taggart* v *Shell (UK) Ltd* 1996 SLT 795; *Girvan* v *Inverness Farmers Dairy (No 2)* 1996 SLT 63.

[69] *Lamont* v *Cameron's Executrix* 1997 SLT 1147; *Kerr* v *Newalls Insulation Co Ltd* 1997 SLT 723.

[70] *Graham* v *Marshall Food Group Ltd* 1998 SLT 1448; *Stirling* v *Norwest Holst Ltd (No 2)* 1998 SLT 1359; *Lightbody* v *Upper Clyde Shipbuilders Ltd* 1998 SLT 884; *Girvan* v *Inverness Farmers Dairy (No 2)* 1998 SLT 21; *Downie* v *Chief Constable, Strathclyde Police* 1998 SLT 8.

[71] *MacLean* v *Lothian and Borders Fire Brigade* 1999 SLT 702; *Duncanson* v *South Ayrshire Council* 1999 SLT 519; *Gallacher* v *Lanarkshire Health Board* 1999 SLT 166.

[72] *Manson* v *Skinner* 2000 SLT (Sh Ct) 161; *Callaghan* v *Southern General Hospital NHS Trust* 2000 SLT 1058; *Grassie* v *MacLaren* 2000 SLT 944.

[73] *McDyer* v *Celtic Football and Athletic Co Ltd (No 2)* 2001 SLT 1387; *Duthie* v *Macfish Ltd* 2001 SLT 833; *Baigent* v *British Broadcasting Corporation* 2001 SLT 427; *Macey-Lillie* v *Lanarkshire Health Board* 2001 SLT 215; *Mackenzie* v *H D Fraser & Sons* 2001 SLT 116.

[74] *Hawkes* v *Wynn* 2002 SLT 1227; *Young* v *Scottish Coal (Deep Mining) Co Ltd* 2002 SLT 1215; *McKenzie* v *Barclay Curle Ltd* 2002 SLT 649; *Wallace* v *Paterson* 2002 SLT 563; *Lewis* v *Richardson* 2002 SLT 272; *McKeown* v *Lord Advocate* 2002 SLT 269.

[75] *Purves* v *Joydisc Ltd* 2003 SLT (Sh Ct) 64; *Armstrong* v *Brake Brothers (Frozen Foods) Ltd* 2003 SLT (Sh Ct) 58; *McKenna* v *British Railways Board* 2003 SLT 1300; *Robson* v *Glasgow City Council* 2003 SLT 788; *D's Parent and Guardian* v *Argyll and Clyde Acute Hospitals NHS Trust* 2003 SLT 511.

[76] *Ross* v *Harper* 2004 SLT 353; *Penny* v *J Ray McDermott Diving International Inc* 2004 SLT 253.

[77] *Haddow* v *Glasgow City Council* 2005 SLT 1219.

[78] Technically four assessments but two arose out of the same accident and were litigated by the same legal teams in the same court – legally the actions were conjoined and for these purposes count as one. These are *Dickson* v *Hastings (No 1)* 2007 SLT (Sh Ct) 161 and

This is evidence of the regular appearance of the JSB in reported cases. Reported cases are those selected for inclusion in the bound volumes of law reports. For every reported case there are many more unreported cases. Looking at unreported cases, the Scottish Courts website "hits"[79] are as follows: two for 1998; three for 1999; seven for 2000; four for 2001; six for 2002; nine for 2003; five for 2004; seven for 2005; nine for 2006; 14 for 2007; and 12 for 2008. This may fairly be said to show increasing use.

At present the JSB guidance is simply used as another source of data, although often awards are close to the range of figures suggested. Sometimes parties dispute which of the JSB categories applies to the facts of the case. The judge has to assess the appropriate category himself.[80] Sometimes only one party will pray the JSB in aid, and that may be the defender seeking to obtain a lower finding.[81] It has been correctly said that obviously the JSB guidelines themselves are published unsupported by authority.[82]

Dickson v *Hastings (No 2)* 2007 SLT (Sh Ct) 164, counting as one, and *Carling* v *WP Bruce* 2007 SLT 743 and *J* v *Fife Council* 2007 SLT 85.

[79] Obvious duplicates are excluded, appeals included.
[80] See, eg, *Lightbody* v *UCS* 1998 SLT 884.
[81] See, eg, *Duncanson* v *South Ayrshire Council* 1999 SLT 519, in which the pursuer argued on authority for £4,000, the defender on JSB for £2,000–£2,500 and Lord Milligan decided on £3,500.
[82] See Lord McCluskey in *McDyer* v *Celtic Football and Athletic Co Ltd (No 2)* 2001 SLT 1387 at 1389.

2. ALTERNATIVE METHODS OF ASSESSMENT

How else might damages be assessed? An infinite number of methods may be postulated. Space demands selection of comparable exercises. The choice here is between (1) the CICA scheme; and (2) the recent Irish reforms. The first shows us how we actually do it here, depending on how and by whom the claimant has been personally injured and the second shows how they do it "next door".[1] If we were examining *liability* itself, some European *ius commune* comparison would be essential, but we are not doing so. That said, an abbreviated survey derived from recent comparative work – on assessment, not liability – is included as (3) "Europe", to provide a more rounded, yet still incomplete, picture of what goes on in the rest of Europe.

CRIMINAL INJURIES COMPENSATION SCHEME

Space precludes a full history.[2] This is a state scheme to compensate victims of crime. There is a direct overlap of function where a person sustains personal injuries at the hands of a criminal. The reason the state system is engaged is that the wrongdoer has gone or has no money. To achieve the compensation function the state uses the taxpayer's money to pay the victim. This differs from the usual compensation case, where the *reality* of most cases (rather than the form) is that the state employs the judge to order an insurance company to use the premium payer's money to compensate the victim.[3] The CICA has always been treated as an exception or as a special case in the traditional books. Rightly so. The CICA is a statutory body. However, in relation to assessment of damages, the CICA scheme is far less exceptional. Indeed, initially it was set up

---

[1] In the sense that Eire is, thanks to Northern Ireland, our only contiguous neighbour.
[2] See P Cane, *Atiyah's Accidents, Compensation and the Law* (7th edn, 2006), pp 304–327.
[3] Or the shareholder's money (or a Name's) if the underwriters have got *their* sums wrong; or some other investors if the insurer has gone bust having got its sums wrong too many times before?

to compute damages according to the common law. As a result, CICB[4] awards were routinely collected and used as extra data in the assessment process. So far as the general taxpayer is concerned, a lot of the cost of the reparation for personal injury part of the judicial process is paid for by insurance[5] and some by the taxpayer.[6] All of the CICA comes from the taxpayer. To save cost, a scheme was introduced to facilitate the calculation of the award. This was far from uncontroversial.[7] For pain and suffering there are 25 bands under the 1996 Scheme, containing *hundreds* of specified injuries. The bands are kept under review by an independent medical panel and the payments were increased in 2001 to take account of inflation.[8] A revised scheme is in force from 2008 but it too is in 25 bands.[9]

There are some other facts from the CICA scheme which are of interest. It is thought that many of the costs and delays in that system are caused by assessment of loss of earnings and cost of care.[10] This might suggest that the use of the fixed bands has taken cost and delay from the system. More importantly, taking account of their injuries, just over half of respondents considered that their award was either very sufficient or sufficient.[11] Of course, as these references are taken from a government study, it ought to be said that just under half of the applicants were *not* happy with their award. So far as cost is concerned, the CICA cases cost a mere £200 to reach a first decision and the average cost of all cases (including those with the loss of earnings and care issues) is about £305.[12]

---

[4] The Criminal Injuries Compensation Board was the informal precursor of the statutory Criminal Injuries Compensation Authority.
[5] Nearly all of the damages and legal costs and some of the court costs.
[6] Some unrecovered legal aid costs; court system costs.
[7] P Duff, "The 1996 Criminal Injuries Compensation Scheme" 1996 SLT (News) 221 at 239; A S Pollock, "Criminal Injuries Compensation: the Tariff" (1996) 40 JLSS 93; I Walker, "Criminal Injuries Compensation: A government betrayal" [1994] JPIL 47. And see *R v Secretary of State for the Home Department* [1995] 2 WLR 464.
[8] *Rebuilding Lives – Supporting Victims of Crime* (Cm 6705, 2005) (henceforth "*RL*") p 17.
[9] The detailed analysis in Appendix 4 is based on the 2001 Scheme but comparison with the 2008 Scheme shows no significant differences to the argument. There are still 25 bands and hundreds of descriptors of injuries: Criminal Injuries Compensation Scheme (2008). In the unlikely but possible situation that a case arises which does not fit a descriptor, there is provision for amending the scheme to include a new descriptor: 2008 Scheme, paras 28 and 29.
[10] *RL*, p 3.
[11] *Ibid*, p 16.
[12] *Ibid*.

So far as the consultation on reforms to the 2001 Scheme is concerned, one of the most interesting for this topic was the idea that only "serious" injuries should be compensated through the CICA. At the time of the study, 57 per cent of the awards were in the £1,000–£2,000 range and, of course, lower amounts have already been put outside the system because there is no award if the claim is not worth £1,000. One of the constant criticisms of the tort system is that it overcompensates some and undercompensates others. Removal of lower cost awards would increase the economic efficiency of the system as a compensatory system. However, generally, reparation has other more constitutional features. Traditionally, it has been thought necessary to mark the infringement of a right with an award. Even in today's most sophisticated times, a conventional award was thought necessary where no legal loss could be found.[13] In the event, after consultation, the CICA scheme was *not* reformed to take account of seriousness[14] and, for example, the £1,000 and £1,250 bands remain.

THE PERSONAL INJURIES ASSESSMENT BOARD IN EIRE

What is a Personal Injuries Assessment Board? The model under consideration is that which has been established in Eire, by virtue of the Personal Injuries Assessment Board Act 2003.[15] It considers (1) a civil action by an employee against his employer for negligence or breach of duty arising in the course of the employee's employment with that employer;[16] a civil action by a person against another arising out of that other's ownership, driving or use of a mechanically propelled vehicle;[17] a civil action by a person against another arising out of that other's use or occupation of land or any structure or building;[18] or a civil action not falling within any of the preceding paragraphs (other than one arising

---

[13] *Rees* v *Darlington Memorial Hospital NHS Trust* [2004] 1 AC 309.
[14] http://www.cjsonline.gov.uk/the_cjs/whats_new/news-3683.html (accessed 8/10/09).
[15] The Act came fully into force on 22 July 2004 by virtue of, *inter alia*, Personal Injuries Assessment Board Act 2003 (Commencement) Order 2004, Personal Injuries Assessment Board Act 2003 (Establishment Day) Order 2004, Personal Injuries Assessment Board Act 2003 (Commencement) (No 2) Order 2004 and Personal Injuries Assessment Board Act 2003 (Commencement) (No 3) Order 2004. It was amended by the Personal Injuries Assessment Board (Amendment) Act 2007 which introduced costs penalties for those not accepting an offer. The PIAB now calls itself the "Injuries Board".
[16] PIABA, s 3(a).
[17] *Ibid*, s 3(b).
[18] *Ibid*, s 3(c).

out of the provision of any health service to a person, the carrying out of a medical or surgical procedure in relation to a person or the provision of any medical advice or treatment to a person).[19] It may be noted that professional negligence cases, other than medical, are capable of inclusion, but that later provisions restrict civil action to ones which claim personal injuries or claim personal injuries and damage to property if both have been caused by the same wrong. The architect may be within the scheme where the wall he designs collapses, breaking a leg and destroying a Rolex watch; not where, through defect of design, the hotel may receive only eight guests instead of the more lucrative 16. *There is no financial limit on claims.* As at the end of February 2005 the PIAB had received 995 employers cases, 978 public liability cases and 1,334 motor accident cases – a total of 3,307 (suggesting that there had been no cases under 3(d)).

How does it operate?

The Irish model does not interfere with the law of liability. In this respect, this is not equivalent to the often discussed New Zealand compensation system.[20] The state is not paying the award and so to this extent it differs from the Criminal Injuries Compensation Scheme. The Irish PIAB instead operates by way of restricting access to the traditional justice system. A claim capable of falling within the scheme must be submitted through the scheme before court action may be raised. The claim is made on a form (which can now be completed online). It contains the usual personal details, a description of the incident, the nature of any injury, an indication of any loss resulting from lost wages or medical expenses, and a medical assessment form from the claimant's treating practitioner. A fee, presently €50, must be paid. The claimant is to get the medical assessment form – and pay for it, albeit with a right to seek recovery of the reasonable and necessary cost which was in fact originally fixed at a mere €150 contribution. After the claim is received by the Board it issues a notice to the respondent. If the respondent writes refusing to consent to an assessment, the claimant is issued with an authorisation allowing him to sue.[21] The claim is valued according to the *Book of Quantum*.[22] Where there is consent or no response, an assessment is made and the parties are free to accept or reject, unless the Board itself considers that

---

[19] PIABA, s 3(d).
[20] Cane, *Accidents*, pp 467–488.
[21] PIABA, s 14.
[22] *Ibid*, s 54(1)(b).

for statutory reasons it is unable to provide an assessment, as where there have been insufficient cases or settlements in relation to the injury.[23] The claimant has 28 days to decide and the respondent 21 days. If the assessment is not for any reason accepted then again an authorisation is issued to permit the matter to proceed through the courts. Thereafter, the assessment effectively becomes binding. A statement may be issued, awarding certain specified expenses. A month later, an order to pay can be issued.

As might be expected, there are many more technical provisions, dealing with multiple defenders, those not of sound mind and those represented by others, to name just a few.

The *Book of Quantum*

As the Board is to act expeditiously, including reaching an assessment within 9 months of a notice of consent to assessment being received, time may well be tight. Provision is made to assist assessment by compelling the Board to compile a document to be known as the *Book of Quantum*. This was established to contain general guidelines as to the amounts that may be awarded or assessed in respect of specified types of injury. Assessment is by officers of the Board who have the power to obtain further assistance. The Board may decline to assess if there is insufficient data in the *Book of Quantum*. It may also decline to assess in various other enumerated circumstances such as the inter-relationship of multiple injuries, psychological harm not amenable to assessment by the means of assessment permitted to the assessors and cases where serious injury would allow for an early trial based on the likely demise of the claimant.

The first version (2004) of the *Book of Quantum*[24] is set out by injured body part "based on the World Health Organisation's International Classification of Diseases version 9 and follows a simple structure of body region/body part/injury type".[25] The body having been carved up, each typical injury is then split into gradations of seriousness: (i) substantially recovered; (ii) significant ongoing; (iii) serious and permanent conditions. To each of these divisions there is allocated a range of awards.[26]

---

[23] PIABA, s 17.
[24] It helpfully begins by shouting in the first sentence that "quantum" means "AMOUNT".
[25] *Book of Quantum*, p 1.
[26] This review has been of the system rather than the amounts awarded. So far as amounts are concerned, the Inner House is likely to treat Irish awards as being too high and the

OTHER EUROPEAN JURISDICTIONS

The following is, of necessity, a brief survey. It derives mainly from the work of the research group of the Pan-European Organisation of Personal Injury Lawyers.[27] The methodology of the basic study is that the reporters reported based upon a standard questionnaire.[28] That questionnaire is reproduced in the published report and it is section 2.2.5.1 of each report which is of interest for this study.[29] For the sake of brevity, a system whereby the judge assesses the non-patrimonial award on a case-by-case basis, perhaps informed by previous decisions, is designated "bespoke" in this book. Some systems make differing use of tables of injury created by medical experts and to which points may be allocated – they differ in application, scope and detail but for these purposes this is signified as a "*barème*" system (absent the use of the correct local term). These were presented alphabetically in the original report but are here set out in four categories (with blurred edges).[30]

Mainly bespoke

Austria utilises a bespoke method. Guidelines exist. Cases are broken into four categories of severity, from light to extreme.[31] A "Table of awards" has been published by a former judge and used as a guideline.[32] While it may be said that there are judicial guidelines, in assessing damages for pain and suffering use is made of "day rates" associated with levels of pain but it is reported that the Supreme Court has disapproved of this method.[33]

---

preference is to compare with England: "Awards in the Republic of Ireland in this field are not helpful. There appears to have been a long tradition in that jurisdiction of making awards in personal injuries cases significantly higher than elsewhere in the British Isles and amongst the highest in Europe" (L P Hamilton, giving the Opinion of the Court in *J* v *Fife Council* 2009 SLT 160 at 165, para 20).

[27] Bona & Mead, *PICE*.

[28] This is the same methodology as the wider Rogers, *Comparative Perspective*. See also McIntosh & Holmes, briefly but effectively mentioned in *J* v *Fife Council* 2009 SLT 160 at 165, para 20.

[29] Bona & Mead, *PICE* at p 13.

[30] Scots courts might take cognisance of such comparative studies. The Inner House declined to follow Irish levels of awards as being too high, under reference to McIntosh & Holmes: *J* v *Fife Council* 2009 SLT 160 at 165, para 20.

[31] See, eg, I Greiter in McIntosh & Holmes at p 202.

[32] I Greitler in Bona & Mead, *PICE* at p 31 *et seq*.

[33] E Karner and H Kozoil in Rogers, *Comparative Perspective* at p 13.

Germany[34] has a bespoke system and without any official guidance but, as in Scotland, guidance is taken from previous cases published privately.[35]

Greece is entirely bespoke.[36]

The Netherlands is essentially a bespoke system, and has no official tables,[37] although there is a respected informal publication providing an overview of the case law.[38] Some guidance can be gained from the review of traffic law revised every 3 years.[39]

Portugal is essentially another bespoke system with no official tables.[40] It has been said that, "injury awards vary significantly even in very similar situations".[41]

Scotland, as has been set out here, is bespoke, with no formal medical table and points system and no official guidance, reliance being placed on at least one very highly regarded text.[42]

Bespoke plus official guidance

Belgium uses a bespoke method.[43] Partly due to divergence between Walloon and Flanders awards, a *National Indicative Table* was adopted in 1997, drawn up by the two associations of judges with assistance from academics, practitioners and insurers; it is for guidance only.[44]

---

[34] P Kuhn in Bona & Mead, *PICE* at pp 224–233; Markesinis, *Compensation* at pp 59–82. For examples, see J Wuppermann in McIntosh & Holmes at pp 337–346.
[35] Hacks *et al*, *Schmerzensgeldbeträge* (20th edn, Munich, 2001), cited in Markesinis, *Compensation*, p 67, n 79; U Magnus and J Fedtke in Rogers, *Comparative Perspective* at p 117.
[36] S Manolkidis in Bona & Mead, *PICE* at pp 253–257; K D Kerameus in Rogers, *Comparative Perspective* at pp 130–132. For examples, see E Tsouroulis, N Domvros and D G Rediadis in McIntosh & Holmes at pp 349–366.
[37] S Lindenbergh and R Verburg in Bona & Mead, *PICE* at pp 367–375. Some examples can be found in M M MacLean in McIntosh & Holmes at pp 445–452.
[38] Published under the auspices of *Verkeersrecht* and discussed by M H Wissink and W H van Broom in Rogers, *Comparative Perspective*.
[39] S Lindenbergh and R Verburg in Bona & Mead, *PICE* at p 373.
[40] A da Costa Basto in Bona & Mead, *PICE* at pp 407–413.
[41] H Dos Santos Pereira in McIntosh & Holmes at p 453. For examples, see *ibid*, pp 457–464.
[42] See also A S Logan in Bona & Mead, *PICE* at pp 425–428 and A H Lockhart, A K Brown and F Thomson in McIntosh & Holmes at pp 465–524.
[43] E de Kezel in Bona & Mead, *PICE* at p 61 *et seq*.
[44] E de Kezel in Bona & Mead, *PICE* at p 61. See also H Cousy and D Droshout in Rogers, *Comparative Perspective* at p 43, who list more informal case law reviews as well, including a looseleaf (n 60).

England and Wales use the bespoke system with the assistance of the *JSB guidelines*.[45]

Finland's system is bespoke, according to one study.[46] In assessing the injury there is a strong presumption in favour of the classifications of the Centre for Legal Security of Health Care. In fixing compensation, comparison is made with the *Table of the Traffic Accident Board*. In another study, only a table and points system appears, either suggesting a system change or emphasising the practical dominance of the tables.[47]

Bespoke plus *barème*

France favours the bespoke method but this moderated by the use of the *barème*.[48] This is used mainly for financial loss. It is used to allocate disability points which may be used by the courts when assessing non-pecuniary loss. A private body attempts to average out in money terms what the various courts have done in relation to the points awarded in the medical reports.[49] So it is a bespoke system coupled with a table and points system. The value of the point increases with the disability rate and decreases with the age of the victim.[50]

Italy has a fundamentally bespoke system but uses a *baremo* scheme for a significant head of non-patrimonial loss based on a points system.[51] Rather like France,[52] various local courts have produced their own tables of allocation of funds to points – a practice approved by the Supreme Court,[53] although perhaps unfortunately judges are able to use any of the regional tables![54] The basic values differ according to age and the value

---

[45] C Garner *et al* in Bona & Mead, *PICE* at 129 *et seq*; Markesinis, *Compensation*, pp 46–59. W V H Rogers in Rogers, *Comparative Perspective* at pp 54–73; M Henké in McIntosh & Holmes at pp 262–301.
[46] P Backström in Bona & Mead, *PICE* at p 166.
[47] H Lagenskiold in McIntosh & Holmes at pp 302–314.
[48] M Cannarsa in Bona & Mead, *PICE* at pp 195–198. Examples can be found in G Honig in McIntosh & Holmes at pp 315–333, although there is no reference there to any table or points. Yet the worked examples feature actual figures rather than a range, so perhaps a table and points have been used in the background.
[49] M Cannarsa in Bona & Mead, *PICE* at p 195.
[50] S Galand-Carval in *Comparative Perspective* at pp 89–91.
[51] M Bona in Bona & Mead, *PICE* at pp 305–325; A A Giorgetti in McIntosh & Holmes at pp 390–418.
[52] The Tribunale of Pisa which adopted a points system is said to have been "inspired by the French experience" (F D Busnelli and G Comandé in Rogers, *Comparative Perspective* at p 146).
[53] M Bona in Bona & Mead, *PICE* at p 321.
[54] *Ibid* at p 322. For a discussion of the national orientation table or TIN, see F D Busnelli and G Comandé in Rogers, *Comparative Perspective* at p 146.

ALTERNATIVE METHODS OF ASSESSMENT 27

of each percentage point increases as the degree of invalidity increases.[55] However, Italy does provide material of some comparative interest.[56] A head of non-pecuniary, indeed non-patrimonial, loss has relatively recently been developed – *danno biologico*. The legislature has intervened to attenuate the new system.[57] It might be wondered whether such intervention was emboldened by the lack of a professional legal history.

Luxembourg's system is said to be akin to the French, being bespoke with tables.[58] While there is no official *barème*, one of the French tables is used, or private *Ravarani* tables.

Spain has a bespoke system outside of road traffic matters but with the assistance of the *baremo*.[59] Of interest is the influence which it is said the "tariffed" road traffic system has on the otherwise bespoke system.[60]

State control

Denmark has a scheme involving statutory controls.[61] The fixed figure stands unless there has been permanent disability, in which case the *Table of the National Board of Industrial Injuries* is used. As has already been indicated, this table is not member (body part)-specific and is simply in six bands of severity.

Ireland has the statutory PIAB, as discussed above, incorporating the *Book of Quantum*. Should a case be diverted out of that system, a bespoke system applies generally.[62]

Norway[63] seems to have quite a restricted system of allowable heads – damage is awarded only in cases of permanent disability.[64] Assessment is based on expert medical evidence which is based on guidelines drawn up

---

[55] M Bona in Bona & Mead, *PICE* at pp 321–322.
[56] This is fully charted throughout the entire text of Markesinis, *Compensation*.
[57] Markesinis, *Compensation*, pp 84–87.
[58] A Kronshagen in Bona & Mead, *PICE* at pp 347–351; R Diederich in McIntosh & Holmes at pp 419–441.
[59] M M Crespo and M M Alcoz in Bona & Mead, *PICE* at pp 444–451.
[60] *Ibid* at p 439; M Pallarés in McIntosh & Holmes at pp 525–548; and see the discussion by M Martín-Casals, J Ribot and J Solé, in Rogers, *Comparative Perspective* at pp 194–195.
[61] B von Eyben and SV Nielsen in Bona & Mead, *PICE* at p 90 *et seq*; J Rasch in McIntosh & Holmes at pp 247–261.
[62] J Schütte in Bona & Mead, *PICE* at pp 266–270; K Delahunt, F Beatty and J G Byrne in McIntosh & Holmes at pp 367–389.
[63] T Sørum in Bona & Mead, *PICE* at pp 390–392.
[64] *Ibid* at p 390. See also P Mitsem in McIntosh & Holmes at pp 588–604. In Mitsem, the examples are calculated under the head "medical disability compensation" only.

by the Norwegian Health Department.[65] There is, however, a degree of tailoring of awards.

Sweden[66] has a statutory system involving insurance boards. Specific tables are used and there is a *barème*-type scheme derived from the Traffic Tables.[67]

---

[65] T Sørum in Bona & Mead, *PICE* at p 391.
[66] B Dufwa in Bona & Mead, *PICE* at pp 469–477; G Dahlström in McIntosh & Holmes at pp 548–564.
[67] The examples given by G Dahlström in McIntosh & Holmes at pp 552–564 employ the heads "pain and suffering" and "disability and detriment".

3. ANALYSIS AND ASSESSMENT OF THE ASSESSMENT PROCESS

WHY ARE PERSONAL INJURY DAMAGES *ASSESSED* AT ALL?

The basic common law position is that the pursuer has been wronged by the defender. In the common law system of justice this fault is a ground for the state intervening to shift assets from the defender to the pursuer. The principle is one of restitution, punishment being thought either primitive or exceptional. Restitution seeks to avoid either over- or under-compensation. The further the result is from equilibrium, the less well the system has performed. It is this point which is perhaps least well understood outside of legal circles. It is one good explanation for why judges and lawyers spend time on this exercise of assessment. They are not, as the cynic might suggest, trying to justify their existence – rather, this is one reason why they exist. Many European systems adopt the fault principle. Many adhere to a principle of full compensation. This is all fine and well with pecuniary losses. However, the idea of compensation for the non-pecuniary aspects of personal injury is inherently defective. It has been noted time and again in Scotland and in England that the exercise is not one of compensation in the sense of the high-level restitution principle at all: "if by somebody's fault I lose my leg and am paid damages, can anyone in his senses say I have had *restitutio in integrum*?"[1]

What appears to have happened is that *substantial* compensation for non-pecuniary harm comes later than liability for non-pecuniary losses. The emphasis on *substantial* is to indicate that a court or a legal system is less likely to be concerned about small additional payments than payments which can be very much larger than many pecuniary loss awards. This would explain why it appears to be the case that mensuration techniques entirely appropriate to working out compensation for financial losses are adopted for other losses too. The losses are all in the one claim. In Scotland, until recently, and as in other systems, a single award of

---

[1] *Admiralty Commissioners* v *SS Valeria* [1922] 2 AC 242 per Lord Dunedin at 248.

damages might be made.² Procedurally there was no opportunity to treat non-pecuniary losses differently.

The clearest analysis of this issue came up in *Rees*,³ because there was in that case, in law, no actionable pecuniary loss: the wrong to the claimant had gone uncompensated below. The House of Lords permitted a conventional award. Accordingly, it is submitted that the time is now right to recognise fully that Scots awards are not compensatory and to stop trying to measure them as if they were. Some form of reform, probably gradual, should be undertaken which sets about establishing satisfactory levels of solace.

Before moving on it may be admitted that there can be found some traces of compensation and that is where it is sometimes suggested in a relatively minor case of an injury that has now healed, that the award should bring good times to compensate the bad times – perhaps related to the cost of a holiday.⁴ But it is submitted that this is really a way of trying to find a value for the lower levels of solace (rather than compensation) absent a percentage scale or tariff. And in any event most systems no longer adhere to this in practice.⁵

As has been mentioned, the Scottish Law Commission included in a discussion paper a question inviting views on the introduction of a tariff for fatal cases.⁶ While it has been accepted that the legal traditions of the two types of claim are different, the tariff issue for fatal claims raises many of the same issues contained in this study. Most significant is the general acceptance in fatal cases that the issue is *not* one of compensation. Yet the process in fatal cases follows closely the "standard" compensatory process. The case for a tariff for fatal cases is made stronger in Scotland in that such has been in operation by statute in England and Wales for some time. However, after consultation the issue was not pursued.⁷ There was a minority who argued strongly in

---

² *Girvan* v *Inverness Farmers Dairy* 1998 SC (HL) 1 at 8–9.
³ *Rees* v *Darlington Memorial Hospital NHS Trust* [2004] 1 AC 309.
⁴ There is a hint of this in Austrian practice: "to find some amenities and facilitations as an equalisation for his suffering and lost joie de vivre": E Karner and H Koziol in Rogers, *Comparative Perspective* at p 7. So too in German law there is the idea of "buying alternative comforts": U Magnus and J Fedtke in Rogers, *Comparative Perspective* at p 112. Also in Belgium, "providing alternative or compensating pleasures to the victim": H Cousy and D Droshout in Rogers, *Comparative Perspective* at p 37. More eloquently, in Spain "los duellos con pan son menos" (mourning with bread is less mourning): M Martín-Casals, J Ribot and J Solé in Rogers, *Comparative Perspective* at p 197.
⁵ W V H Rogers, "Comparative Report" in Rogers, *Comparative Perspective* at p 253.
⁶ SLC, *Wrongful Death*, paras 3.56–3.66.
⁷ SLC Report, paras 3.51–3.52.

favour of a tariff – they recognised that the award was not compensatory, that a tariff might allow a quicker payment and that levels would not ossify if the Scottish Ministers might adjust amounts.[8] However, it was noted that the present system works and there is no great demand for change.[9] That is correct. These points (it works [after a fashion] and there is no demand for change) may also be applied to the point of this book. However, responding to that in defence of this exercise, the first point is to generate demand for change – until people outside of the legal system know what is going on, there will seldom be demand for improvement. On the second point, while it is true too that the fatal system works, the question is whether it works as well and as efficiently as it might. In any event, the important difference between fatal cases and the cases considered in this book is that there are many thousands more non-fatal cases and so the efficiency gains are greater. By far the strongest point made against a fatal cases tariff was this: "Under a tariff system, the deceased's relative would be entitled to the payment regardless of the quality of their relationship with the deceased. If the courts were to retain discretion to depart from the level of the tariff to take into account exceptional cases, this would undermine the whole rationale for having a tariff system in the first place."[10] There is no place here to review the whole unsatisfactory and slightly unpleasant issue of examining the quality of relationship with a person who is deceased and cannot complain that the claimant might be exaggerating the quality of that relationship. So it may be conceded that if Scots law wants to keep doing this then it does makes a fatal cases tariff more difficult.[11] That argument, the strongest deployed against the fatal tariff, does not apply to any non-fatal tariff where relationship is not in issue.

---

[8] SLC Report, para 3.50. The present author took advantage of the work being done on this book to be one of that minority!

[9] *Ibid*, para 3.52.

[10] *Ibid*, para 3.51.

[11] Although not impossible. It could be met, and some unpleasant proof and excessive cost avoided, perhaps by having a tariff *with categories within the bands*. Personally, three bands would suffice: poor relationship; usual relationship; and excellent relationship. This might encourage settlement by defenders where there is clear evidence of living together or regular visiting and Twittering or whatever, and discourage extravagant claims and settlement for the lower figure by those claimants demonstrably off the Christmas card list. Others might prefer five bands to include "next to nothing" at the very bottom and to move "excellent" to the highest and interpose "good" at band 4. Can any judge or juror truly measure the now deceased's relationship in any finer scale?

HUMAN RIGHTS

Human rights issues do not immediately come to mind in relation to this general topic. However, if, following the arguments in this volume, there were reform imposing a tariff of some kind, an injured person after reform involving a tariff might receive less than in a case before reform. Some personal injury lawyers in Europe see any attempt to remove entitlement from a person to claim damages or "full damages" resulting from injury to their family member as potentially infringing.[12] So "human rights" is said to be one answer to the question posed above – why are damages assessed at all? Despite mention of human rights, what is still absent is any convincing demonstration of how such a challenge would be fully argued. The principal argument against these general human rights points is that made above – that the issue of total reparation or full compensation simply does not arise in this context. It is in fact conventional awards that are made (albeit the quantifying of the convention is more or less complex from system to system). In that the awards are conventional there is no human rights point. If there were a good human rights point, citizens from states which award no or low non-pecuniary damages, for, say, non-criminal pain and suffering, might have been expected to take this point. One fully argued paper has been published since Bona & Mead, *PICE* and has examined ECHR cases.[13] The first case considered therein is *Öneryildiz* v *Turkey*,[14] arising out of the death of nine of the claimant's relatives and the loss of his illegal slum house. In Turkey the claimant received €2,077 in pecuniary damages and €210 for household goods. In addition the negligent mayors were fined €9.70. The ECHR awarded the claimant €45,250 in non-pecuniary damages and €33,750 to each of his sons. The initial award was said to have been of a questionable amount. It was held that, among other infringements, Art 1 Protocol 1 ECHR (Right to property) had been violated. The second case discussed is *Maurice* v *France*,[15] which was a case by parents in respect of a child born with a genetic defect, born because a test which would have allowed abortion was mixed up and the pregnancy declared healthy. The heart

---

[12] See, eg, M Bona, *Bona & Mead*, *PICE* at p 289 *et seq*; M Bona, "Comparative Report", *ibid* at p 552 *et seq*.

[13] J Beer, "Compensation for Personal Injury and Human Rights: The European Court of Human Rights Monitors the Quality of Compensation Law in the Contracting States", PEOPIL Bulletin July 2006, 3–7.

[14] Chamber Judgment, 18 June 2002; Grand Chamber, 30 November 2004.

[15] 11810/03, 6 October 2005.

of the case, though, is that as a result of other litigation, the French Government had decided to legislate to close off wrongful birth cases and restrict parents' claims. The legislation applied to all pending cases which had not come to a final decision. The point before the European Court of Human Rights was that Art 1 of Protocol 1 ECHR (Right to property) had been violated. It was held that it had been. The claim to compensation was to be regarded as a possession. The third case is *Hatton* v *UK*[16] which is naturally familiar to UK lawyers. The claimants lost their case that increased flying was a breach of their Art 8 right to respect for a private and family life. However, reliance is placed on the finding that Art 13 (Effective remedies) had been violated because the English court had been restricted in its consideration of the private and family life rights. The fourth case relied upon is not from the ECtHR but from the Amsterdam Court of Appeal: *Baardman* v *Ns*.[17] Here, a lady was injured when her arm was trapped by two sliding doors closing on a train. The Netherlands Railway admitted liability but claimed to be entitled to a statute limiting damages in such a case. It is reported that the Court accepted that the right to compensation in full is protected by Art 1 of Protocol 1 (Right to property) but that a balanced cap could be justifiable. In this case it was not justified, and the damages had to be paid in full.

Perhaps the strongest of these cases, in this context, is *Maurice*. In that case an *existent* right was removed for the purposes of damages reform. That does not usually happen in the UK. In this particular field legislation will usually refer to causes of action arising after commencement. Any tariff would probably be introduced in such a way as not to affect cases where the causes of action had arisen before the introduction of any tariff (whether or not the tariff is higher or lower than ordinary awards).

Baardman appears to proceed on acceptance that there is some generalised right in Art 1 Protocol 1. If, however, the law does not provide for damages in a given situation, it appears from *Maurice* that there is no possession in the first place. *Hatton* is outside the field of ordinary personal injury and the decision did not relate to full compensation, only condemning the judicial review procedure. *Öneryildiz* is also distinguishable from ordinary personal injury cases in that the claimant's heritable property was destroyed.

Scots lawyers are unlikely to miss any relevant ECHR points. There has already been a substantial challenge utilising ECHR jurisprudence in

---

[16] Chamber 2, October 2001; Grand Chamber, 8 July 2003.
[17] Amsterdam Court of Appeal, 12 August 2004, LJN AR2333.

this general context, albeit that the challenge was by *defenders* unhappy at a process that allowed an uninstructed jury to assess damages![18] The Gill Report took into account discussions of possible human rights challenges to potential reforms introducing compulsory ADR.[19]

Accordingly, while it is possible that where there is a right to *compensation*, the ECHR might be engaged, it is hard, at present, to be convinced that a transparent system for liquidating *conventional* awards would or could infringe the ECHR.

TRANSPARENCY AND INFORMATION

The present system is defective in relation to its transparency. As discussed above, for some time information was handled only by an elite group of legal professionals. Now there is more information available to more professionals, albeit the more that cases settle, in the absence of any reliable register of settlements, the less information there is available. It remains the case that, as in any bespoke system, a client cannot be advised of a likely settlement figure, although a professional should be able to give a broad potential range. Because this advice requires access to case law and the ability to manipulate it, quantum cannot properly be computed by untrained lay persons. An official tariff system of some sort becomes accessible to all citizens and may be used by persons with few formal legal skills, as with the CICA scheme and the PIAB *Book of Quantum*. The whole matter of how much a client might expect to receive becomes much more easy to explain to that client by pointing at a table as opposed to explaining the system set out herein and exemplified in Appendices 1–3. Wrath at the amount being too little can be directed towards the democratic authorities instead of a judicial system doing its best to operate an inherited historical system.

Information deficit as danger

There is a theme which runs through the project: the flow of information. An information gap has been identified. But it is likely to come as a surprise to those who do not specialise in personal injury litigation that the gap *is* being filled. Unfortunately, it is being filled by a private system created for the benefit of insurers. There exists a computerised expert system, called Colossus, which provides information privately and

---

[18] *Heasman v J M Taylor & Partners* 2002 SC 326; 2002 SLT 451.
[19] Gill Report, vol I, Annex C, paras 48–53.

secretly to insurers in order to help them settle cases at the lowest possible level. It may be accepted that the sheriff in the East may not know of awards in the West unless advised on the basis of detailed research. The Markesinis, *Compensation* study carries an appendix showing the divergence of awards across the various Italian states, making it clear that divergence is an operational hazard of a bespoke system such as our own. While judicial damages assessment is, in the nicest sense, parochial, the insurance industry is global. Colossus can be encountered in the literature as far back as 1992.[20] At that time it was found in New South Wales and that may in fact be its home of origin. It started as an answer to some of the very problems identified in this book. Claims were assessed in various ways. A detailed study of settlements by insurers showed a variation of 100 per cent in assessments by less experienced claims handlers. The insurers were paying out too much. It was established as a traditional computer expert system and had the help of a retired expert judge for expert input.

Only insiders know how this proprietary system works. The details from 1992 show that it is (or was) no rough tariff but is moulded to meet a fairly bespoke system – the assessor may have to answer up to 700 questions; it has built-in medical information as to how long it takes for certain injuries to heal; and provides a medical encyclopaedia to help. For common law cases it worked on the basis of taking the highest award and discounting according to the expert system analysis.

It is still robot-like but alarming in that way in which chess computers are now smarter than humans.[21] In the late 1980s Colossus offered too little (compared with courts) for whiplash, applying its scaling-down formulae. Probably the computer was right and previous awards had been too high, but it had to be adjusted to match the proclivity of the courts for paying more for whiplash than the overall picture (if known) would indicate. In the 1992 analysis it transpired that the summary report used for settlement would be given to the claimant's lawyer and even that sometimes the claimant's lawyer would be allowed to input data to have a consultation of their own. The 1992 study was about general damages

---

[20] G Greenleaf, "A Colossus come to judgment: GIO's expert system on general damages" (1993) 67 ALJ 220.
[21] Garry Kasparov, the then highest-rated chess player of all time, was defeated by a computer program: D King, *Kasparov v Deeper Blue* (1997). The challenge for modern chess computer designers is "artificial stupidity" – to make the program play such that it might conceivably be beaten while still offering a challenge: W R Hartson, "Artificial Stupidity" in D F Beal (ed), *Advances in Computer Chess 4* (1986).

which is similar in conception to the element of solatium which is being discussed here. Colossus worked for the insurance industry – there was 80 per cent deviation when human assessors were tested and only 15 per cent when Colossus was tested. Better, offers had been going up at 14 per cent per year; after Colossus, they did not go up at all.

Colossus now affects the claims of Scottish claimants. The non-specialist profession was initially alerted by a series of advertisements by a leading firm of claims lawyers.[22] Since then there has been a fuller analysis by a leading personal injury lawyer and it brings the Colossus story up to date.[23] Conway points out that Norwich Union, the UK's largest insurer, uses it and that Groupama signed a 5-year deal in 2007 for use of the system.[24] He records US experience – again in the early days of 1992 when Allstate Corporation was able to move from paying out 87 cents for each premium dollar to 43 cents. He notes that the system contains only its own settlement figures – removing the transaction further from the simulation of a real court outcome: "In the long run, the house always wins. And it keeps its own records, justifying further lowball strategies."[25] There is no longer the "give and take" of settlement discussions.[26] Another very experienced litigator sought and obtained quantitative data on the issue and found that of 480 cases the total of pre-litigation offers amounted to £2,068,486.[27] When litigated, the damages amounted to £4,892,292.[28] It was thought, based on those figures, that Colossus could be behind the unrealistically low figures offered.[29] So, without a doubt, if these figures are representative, insurers appear to be coming in far too low to the detriment of claimants and forcing pressure on the overall court system.

The medical information

It has been seen that some European systems use a table and points system – the *barème* model. The location (and value) of the claim depends upon the medical points awarded. Such systems are attractive in providing

---

[22] Eg "You don't have to settle for what the computer says": advertisement, JLSS, vol 52, no 1, January 2007.
[23] Conway, *Colossus*.
[24] *Ibid*, p 14.
[25] *Ibid*, p 16.
[26] *Ibid*.
[27] G Garrett, "A Breach of Protocol", 2008 (Feb) JLSS 14 at 15 (henceforth "Garrett, *Protocol*").
[28] *Ibid*.
[29] *Ibid*, p 16 (also entirely endorsing Conway's views).

harmony in jurisdictions where there is no simple central court and the danger of different treatment of medically similar cases, such as France,[30] or Italy.[31]

At present in Scotland, the source of the medical information varies. There is not even a single common medical witness. On the traditional adversarial model, parties obtain their own evidence. Recent procedural reforms, directed to encouraging settlement where it is possible, have encouraged the claimant to ensure that a medical report is lodged if it is to be founded upon, so that the defender can decide whether it is adequate for their purposes or whether to obtain their own report. A voluntary pre-action protocol negotiated between the Law Society of Scotland and leading insurers provides for the exchange of medical information. Many reports may be obtained at some cost during a claim. The present system is partially defective in some cases. A case run at low cost may be run with an inadequate medical report. Many cases are run with a report from the claimant's own doctor – it would not be unnatural for a physician treating a person to be optimistic as to prognosis. Equally, some cases are delayed by the need to obtain information from doctors who are busy with their prime task of trying to make people well again. It is in fact left to the trier of fact to try to determine what the final medical information says about the claimant's condition before moving on to assessment. The Gill Report recommends making the existing voluntary protocols compulsory[32] *and* extending them to all personal injury claims, not just those up £10,000 as at present.[33] This is certainly an opportunity to start to improve this aspect of the process.

The English system is now directed towards the use of a single appointed expert, although the adversarial system continues to challenge such modernising case management.[34] The CICA decides whether or not to obtain a medical report. The PIAB accepts a medical report from the "treating practitioner" in the first instance but it encourages the use of a standard form and provides guidance to the medical community on what is expected.

---

[30] S Galand-Carval in *Comparative Perspective* at p 90.
[31] See the appendix of regional awards in Markesinis, *Compensation*.
[32] Gill Report, Chapter 8, paras 33–34.
[33] *Ibid*, Chapter 8, para 36.
[34] A clear example of this is the struggle by defenders to try to be able to call their own medical experts in cases of low-velocity road traffic collisions: *Kearsley* v *Klarfeld* [2005] EWCA Civ 1510; [2006] 2 All ER 303; *Casey* v *Cartwright* [2006] EWCA Civ 1280; [2007] 2 All ER 78.

There is a given amount of medical information available in any case but it is the legal assessment process which determines what is required. At present our system of medical information gathering, if utilised to the full, does meet the rather luxurious bespoke assessment system. If the system changes, so too can the nature and scope of the medical information which is required. As the CICA system shows, if the assessment system is streamlined, then the medical evidence need only be directed to determining into which category the case falls.

This topic is discussed in more detailed under the topic of "European harmonisation" below.

WHY IS THERE NO TARIFF?

The absence of a tariff has come about in an unconscious way. There is nothing against some form of tariff on historical grounds. Historically, some tariffs have existed in the distant past – most notably the table of the price of blood and injuries[35] – but it is not clear to what extent they were ever in effect.[36] It seems that by the 16th century the original Scots remedy of assythment, the principal remedy for wrongful death, was not fixed but often negotiated by the parties or modified by the judge.[37] By the time of the 17th century, assythment is still at large, although the ability and estate of the offender are still factors.[38] There is nothing un-Scottish about a tariff. The tariff was abolished not by native Scots but by Edward I.[39]

There may be an irony. It seems that the award for pain and suffering (and on death) may have come from practitioners sweeping away the old Roman law (which did not compensate for injury to a freeman) because of their desire to adhere to customary or Germanic law which provided *fixed* sums of money for comfort.[40] As explained above, a tariff does actually exist in Scotland now – the CICA scheme.

---

[35] *Regiam Majestatem*, Book IV, 40 (Skene, edited and translated by Lord Cooper, Stair Society, vol 11).
[36] D M Walker, *A Legal History of Scotland*, vol II (2001), p 618.
[37] D M Walker, *A Legal History of Scotland*, vol III (2001), p 725.
[38] D M Walker, *A Legal History of Scotland*, vol IV (2001), p 697.
[39] D McKenzie and R Evans-Jones, "The Development of Remedies for Personal Injuries and Death" in *The Civil Law Tradition in Scotland*, R Evans-Jones (ed), Stair Society Supplementary vol 2, 1995, p 284.
[40] R Zimmermann, *The Law of Obligations: Roman Foundations of the Civilian Tradition* (1996), p 1026. (Probably similar to our own solatium.) Here it must be conceded that Zimmermann notes Feenstra as alluding to a potential strand through Grotius to

ANALYSIS AND ASSESSMENT 39

It *is* the case that the profession considers that there is no prospect of there being a tariff which can be established by the judiciary itself.[41] Professor Walker's influential book, *The Law of Damages in Scotland*, cited *dicta* in *Elliot* v *Glasgow Corporation* which, while not using the word "tariff", was clear that awards should not go to help forming a "proportional scale or standard".[42] He goes on to add that "a tariff" was also disapproved in *Kelly* v *Glasgow Corporation*.[43] Of course both cases, stretching back over half a century and with antecedents going back even further, are decided in the context of jury trial. All they really decide is that cases should not usually exceed double the correct amount and that the correct amount is deduced from other cases. Yet Professor Walker's use is fair, for while no tariff is found to exist in *Kelly*, the suggestion is that it could have been an error to have applied one. In discussing the various approaches, White & Fletcher,[44] cite[45] a *dictum* of Lord Guthrie in *McCallum* v *Paterson*.[46] This too was in the context of an appeal against a jury trial (by way of a motion for a new trial). This sort of comment is in the context of judges being compelled to respect the position of the jury. Judges have not been able to take charge of the process because, politically, juries are entrenched in the system. There is no great foundation case nor series of cases deciding to favour a bespoke method over a tariff and these cases against any tariff are, it is submitted, "polluted" by the politically entrenched place of civil jury trial.

It will be recalled that the main reason the Gill Review decided to retain civil jury trial was to calibrate damages awards. While, arguably, jury awards now achieve this to some extent in the realm of the rarer fatal cases, it does not do this in any meaningful way in ordinary personal injury cases as there are simply far too few relevant cases. A calibrating system is needed when measurement is difficult and under this model it is necessary to await a suitable case involving the relevant injury to happen at all and to reach all the way to a jury trial for calibration. In any event, if the fixing of conventional awards were transferred to a Commissioner,

---

restitution. In that event, there *is* an argument for seeking to assess at large and if this were thought determinative, it would require investigation, not least in view of Stair's great debt to Grotius.

[41] *Shaher* v *British Aerospace Flying College Ltd* 2003 SC 540 at 543 (a fatal case).
[42] Per LP Clyde at 148–149.
[43] 1951 SC (HL) 15 at 19.
[44] R M White and M J Fletcher, *Delictual Damages* (2000).
[45] *Ibid* at p 90.
[46] 1969 SC 85 at 90.

there would be removed one of the perceived strongest reasons for keeping civil jury trial at all.

COST

It is possible to make an argument that because people do not themselves purchase insurance in respect of non-patrimonial personal injury losses, they themselves do not assign any value to such "losses" and that accordingly the whole system could be abolished. That has been considered, discussed and rejected in one of the leading European studies, mainly on the (good) grounds that the law is not logic alone and that everyone does it.[47] Accordingly, no such suggestion is taken forward here, rather the less dramatic matter of cost reduction.

Very large sums of money are involved in compensation claims. So much so that in England and Wales the industry has had to be regulated.[48] A full, but dated, survey of the compensatory effects of the whole tort system is available, together with statistics and economic data courtesy of the work of the Pearson Commission which is still discussed today.[49] More up-to-date information is available from various sources should it be considered that reform would be indicated. For example, the leading current text, based on figures provided by the Compensation Recovery Unit, indicates that in a recent year there were 400,000 successful tort claims for personal injury and death arising out of road accidents;[50] 250,000 successful workplace injury and disease cases;[51] and many more from public liability claims.[52] A government report produced prior to the (mainly English) Compensation Act 2006 estimated the cost of the whole tort compensation system at over £7 billion.[53] Most recently it has been reported, after a study of two million bodily injury cases, that the number of awards paid out by UK motor insurers alone rose by 9.5 per cent per annum between 1996 and 2006 with the number of claims

---

[47] W V H Rogers, "Comparative Report" in Rogers, *Comparative Perspective* at p 249.
[48] Compensation Act 2006.
[49] Royal Commission on Civil Liability and Compensation for Personal Injury (Pearson Commission) (Cmnd 7054, 3 vols, 1978).
[50] Cane, *Accidents*, pp 214–216.
[51] *Ibid*, pp 216–218.
[52] *Ibid*, p 219.
[53] Noted in Cane, *Accidents* at p 194, n 53, citing the Government's *Compensation Bill Final Regulatory Impact Assessment* (2005), para 2.10 (relating to 2004): available at www.dca.gov.uk/legist/compensation.pdf (accessed 8/10/09).

rising at a rate of 3 per cent per annum.[54] Costs rose 840 per cent over 20 years.[55]

At the time of Pearson, 55 per cent of the money went to the injured and 45 per cent in administration. The Criminal Injuries Compensation Authority has reported that their cases cost £200 to a first decision. Overall, including cases with pecuniary and care issues, CICA cases cost £350. Of motor insurance premiums, 10 per cent is said to be for legal costs.[56] For motor claims insurers say they pay lawyers 43 pence for every pound of compensation that goes to claimants,[57] which is clearly very much worse than the Pearson figure because there will be other administration costs apart from legal costs. More broadly, for England, the Department for Constitutional Affairs recently indicated that "costs can often exceed compensation sometimes by a considerable amount. Cases with a value of less than £2,000 have incurred claimant costs of between £4,500 and £7,000",[58] although these figures are inflated, in contrast to Scotland, by the prevalence in England of "after the event" insurance premiums which are chargeable against the wrongdoer.[59] For Scotland, the Gill Review recognised that there was little published research on the cost of litigation in Scotland.[60] The Review utilised consultation as a way of obtaining *some* data on the matter.[61] One data set of 93 Court of Session actions showed a median ratio of court expenses to award or settlement figure of 136:100.[62] That means the process cost more than the award. Value banding analysis established what has been found elsewhere, namely that the ratio of cost to damages gets worse the lower the amount.[63] This applied too in the sheriff court sample. In cases of settlements under £50,000 down to £20,000, the total costs ratio was 101:100. In cases under £20,000 the ratio was 202:100, that is over twice the value to the claimant.[64]

---

[54] International Underwriting Association and Association of British Insurers, Fourth Bodily Injury Awards Study, press release, 08.10.07. ("FBIAS").
[55] *Ibid*.
[56] *Ibid*.
[57] *Ibid*.
[58] Department for Constitutional Affairs, *Case track limits and the claims process for personal injury claims*, Consultation Paper, CP 8/07 20/04/2007 ("DCA-CP"), para 52.
[59] DCA-CP, para 53.
[60] Gill Report, Chapter 4, para 109.
[61] *Ibid*, Chapter 4, para 109.
[62] *Ibid*, Chapter 4, para 111. The cost figure, it is accepted, might be understated.
[63] *Ibid*, Chapter 4, para 113 and related tables in Annex C.
[64] *Ibid*, vol 1, Annex C, Table 5b.

The PIAB wrote in the following terms in 2006 – which, if valid, is support for a meaningful context for this investigation on other than pure intellectual grounds: "resolution of cases through PIAB involves a fixed cost regime averaging €1,330 per claim. This represents at least an 88 per cent saving compared to the older litigation system where legal costs were invariably a percentage of the award or settlement regardless of what was involved in the case. In its early stages of operation this means that PIAB delivered savings of over €24m by reducing the overhead costs traditionally incurred to deliver compensation entitlements. For a full year's operations the projected saving is €48m over all classes of liability and motor injury cases, without even factoring in the upfront resolution of claims facilitated by the very existence of PIAB but on which no formal assessments proceed".[65]

Claims are paid by, among others, the state (through taxes), by local government (through taxes), by the private sector and by private individuals.[66] Well-known studies demonstrate that payment of damages may affect behaviour, although not always predictably,[67] and that the enormously widespread practice of insurance distorts the picture that appears in the law reports. Such studies also make the significant point that the least efficient payments are small payments.[68] Non-pecuniary personal injury damages often represent the smallest payments.[69] Efficiency in respect of this part of the damages industry could have a beneficial effect greater than other cases which generate higher damages payments. Of course, it will be worth gaining an insight as to where efficiency gains are transmitted. There may be more for the halt and the lame, or perhaps for shareholders of insurance companies or a reduction on the burden on the taxpayer. In the short run, a decrease in transaction costs (principally the cost of law) should at least prevent increased insurance costs. Insurance costs are especially relevant for Scotland which as a small jurisdiction may *some day* face similar problems to those of Eire whose reforms are said to have been generated by the small size of

---

[65] Introduction by the Chairperson to the statutory cost–benefit analysis (PIAB, 2006); B Hogan, *A Cost–Benefit Analysis of the PIAB 2006* (PIAB, 2006); http://www.injuriesboard.ie/eng/Forms_and_Publications/Corporate_Publications/A_Cost_Benefit_Analysis_of_the_Personal_Injuries_Assessment_Board.pdf (accessed 8/10/09).
[66] See P S Atiyah, *The Damages Lottery* (1997), Chapter 5, "Who Pays?".
[67] G Calabresi, *The Costs of Accidents: A legal and economic analysis* (1970).
[68] Cane, *Accidents*, p 398.
[69] Latest information from England is that the majority of personal injury claims are for amounts less than £5,000 and the number of cases there runs into several hundred thousands: DCA-CP, para 55.

the insurance pool.⁷⁰ "Some day" because it may be the case that Scottish damages awards under the Scottish legal system at present are met from a UK insurance pool – at least in respect of road traffic and employer's liability which involve compulsory insurance under UK law.

So there are opportunities to improve the system for all. As matters stand, with the information deficit and a lack of democratic involvement, there are threats. It has been suggested that the inflexibility of Colossus puts an unnecessary strain on the court system – if parties cannot negotiate, the informed claimants' lawyer must litigate. Thus it is reported that one defenders' agent had to run 20 proofs – because the computer fixed a lower figure than might be expected by the courts – and lost them all, adding more cost to the overall system.⁷¹

EUROPEAN HARMONISATION

It is clear from Bona & Mead, *PICE*, that complete European harmonisation is far off. At the high level of discussion about liability, there is meaningful European work at the doctrinal level.⁷² In due course that might "trickle down" to the quantification of these losses. The main contribution of high-level work would be rationalisation of the heads of compensable loss. However the value of the various European studies is that there is a case to be made for a "bottom up" approach as well. From the review of European systems it can be seen that there exists quite a range of options but some common themes. Scotland is not at all alone in having a bespoke system and no formal guidance whatsoever. Many systems utilise a formal *barème* to identify the injuries being discussed. Many systems have some formal or informal guidance on quantification. Some combine the *barème* with something else which translates that

---

[70] Panel of Eminent Persons, *Review of the Law of Negligence Final Report*, October 2002 ("Ipp Report").
[71] Conway, *Colossus*, p 16.
[72] Notable is the European Group on Tort Law, an extensive comparative research project which was formerly known as the "Tilburg Group" from its origins in a 1993 working group called together by Jaap Spier, at that time Professor at the University of Tilburg in the Netherlands. It has published its *Principles of European Tort Law* at http://www.egtl.org/ (accessed 8/10/09). See the formal version: European Group of Tort Law, *Principles of European Tort Law: Text and Commentary* (SpringerWien, New York, 2005). Perhaps more influential for the future might be the tort/delict provisions of the *Draft Common Frame of Reference* which provides a full "code". The academic draft of this document has been published: *Interim Outline Edition – Draft Common Frame of Reference (DCFR), Principles, Definitions and Model Rules of European Private Law*, Von Bar, Clive *et al* eds (Sellier, 2008). A full commentary will appear in late 2009.

medical source into money, usually by using points. In some systems, the courts have little control, the state playing a greater role. In some systems development has come initially through road traffic schemes or is related in some way to such systems.

How this can work can be seen by looking at a relevant rule from the *Principles of Tort Law*:

> "In cases of personal injury, non-pecuniary damage corresponds to the suffering of the victim and the impairment of his bodily or mental health. In assessing damages (including damages for persons having a close relationship to deceased or seriously injured victims) similar sums should be awarded for objectively similar losses."[73]

One of the members of the Group has in fact published a more detailed paper summarising work of a group of jurists which addressed the way in which the objectivity and similarity points can be met.[74] The idea was to identify a core which could be harmonised and given practical effect.

> "5.2.1. The damage to be considered as the *main feature* must derive from a harm that can be verified and quantified in percentage terms, and it must be possible to evaluate and quantify in monetary terms on the basis of a table of compensation. It is the non-economic damage par excellence: its qualification as an independent and priority damage, in the opinion of the working Group, represents the real basis for a European model for the rationalisation of the compensation of non-economic damages. The need for uniformity takes precedence over the need for personalisation (which must not, however, be completely neglected).
>
> 5.2.2 The damages to be considered *at a secondary level* are special damages in two ways: they can result from harm caused to a person – considered in a completely general manner as a harm having consequences of a physical and psychic nature – which do not necessarily imply harm has been caused to the physical and/or psychic integrity that is quantifiable in percentage terms (for example: a linear scar without associated pathology); correctly, they concern some particular aspects of the harm which tend to diminish the *quality of life*. They are aspects that are medically verifiable and/or explainable (and which can, if required, be classed on the basis of a scale of seriousness), but which cannot be quantified in percentage terms; their appreciation cannot be translated into monetary terms obtained by applying a table of compensation. The need for personalisation here takes

---

[73] Title V1, Chapter 10, Section 3, Art. 10:301, (3).
[74] F D Busnelli, "Summary report of work effected by the Jurists Group, Trier, 8–9 June 2000", Institute for European Traffic Law website, http://www.eu-traffic-law.org/. See "documents" and then "initiatives" (accessed 8/10/09).

precedence over the need for uniformity (which must not, however, be completely neglected). The various special damages have been standardised by medical science. The working Group of Legal Medicine Specialists has summarised the results of this standardisation by formulating a list of special damages including: *aesthetic harm; sexual harm, harm to leisure activities; exceptional pain and suffering.*"[75]

It is submitted that this is feasible and probably desirable. Scots law recognises such heads and would have no difficulty in adapting to such a system. While there is no guarantee that all of Europe will move in this direction, the existence of the *barème* in many states suggests that it is a possible, perhaps likely, direction.

A further important development in this direction is the production of a proposed European disability rating scale.[76] It will be recalled that France and Italy have already had to deal with the problem of many courts trying to achieve the same end. The preamble to the extensive European disability rating scale considers many of the same themes as this book:

"The effects which cause prejudice to individuals affect human beings in a sphere of activity which is roughly the same for everyone. The same effects thus have virtually identical repercussions on everyday life: it makes sense to assume that they can be assessed on the same basis. They lend themselves to scale based assessment. In practice the current system is satisfactory despite its imperfections and allows for assessment which is relatively reproducible because, whether overtly or not, it is scale-based. Why do the experts in most EU Member States not make do with a simple description? Because the transposition of this description by the person deciding on compensation is in effect an interpretation. And any interpretation can mean alteration, especially where the description given by an expert in one country is used by the decision-maker in another country: it is dangerous to underestimate the problems of language and specialist terminology. It would thus seem a good idea to aim for synthesis and precision, rating specific sequelae by a percentage figure and an explanation: *'expertise means listening, observing, measuring, understanding and then explaining so that others can understand'*. The system of percentage ratings needs a set scale so that there can be equality and fairness: the same sequelae mean the same rating and the same compensation. The most obvious deficiency of existing

---

[75] *Op cit*, p 12.
[76] Rothley Group on the European Scale, *Proposed European disability rating scale*, produced under the auspices of Confédération Européenne d'Experts en Evaluation et en Réparation du Dommage Corporel (CEREDOC) http://www.ceredoc.eu/ An English translation was available from Institute for European traffic Law website: http://www.eu-traffic-law.org/"Documents-European Barème" (accessed 8/10/08 but could not be accessed recently).

scales is that they are not scientifically designed: they are a fusion of rating accepted by the courts' 'conventional scales'. But they have the virtue of evolving in line with the advances achieved in treatment, rehabilitation, imaging and measuring methods and our knowledge of the difficulties faced by victims of trauma."[77]

The paper goes on to explain the need for a European scale. It develops the points made in relation to medical information:

"Doctors impute symptoms to causes, provide objective opinions and quantify, without exceeding the limits of their own specific areas of competence, in the full knowledge that the complexity of the human being cannot always fit adequately into the framework defined by lawyers. The job of the medical assessor is on the one hand to quantify impairments of the human person which can be identified and/or explained in medical terms, and on the other hand to give a specialist opinion on a set list of any types of individual prejudice suffered. Assessment looks at disabilities (impairments of physical and/or mental integrity) which are medically identifiable and thus measurable."[78]

Compared with the present Scottish system, this would encourage specialist independent reports. It would facilitate the use of any tariff or guidelines. The learned editors of *McEwan & Paton* or *Bennett* could map their data to the tables (after the doctors have agreed to use it).

Pressure for European harmonisation is as likely to come from the bottom up as from the top down. The insurance industry probably has an interest in there being a common scale – although, for the good of the claimants of Europe, it might be better if it did not repose within the bowels of a private expert system. The Pan-European Organisation of Personal Injury Lawyers opposed the proposed European *barème*.[79] It has been seen that road traffic cases have often led the way in developments and the fact that road traffic insurance is, to an extent, harmonised might lead to further upward pressure. Insurers have discovered, for example, that the UK paid approximately £150 million more than *the rest of Europe* (emphasis added) in whiplash cases and a total for whiplash of £1.25 billion.[80] Whiplash claims constituted 17

---

[77] *Op cit*, p 5.
[78] *Ibid*, p 6.
[79] PEOPIL's Response to the Recommendations to the Commission on a European Disability Scale, January 2004: http://www.peopil.com/peopil/userfiles/file/Bareme MedicalTablesHarmonisationofdamagesJan2004.pdf (accessed 8/10/09).
[80] A study by Allianz Cornhill summarised in *Claims Management*, vol 1, issue 6, April–May 2007, p 13.

per cent of claims as opposed to 9 per cent in France. Whiplash claims made up 76 per cent of bodily claims in the UK whereas in France the amount was below 3 per cent.[81]

LESSONS OF RECONSTRUCTION: RECONSTRUCTING THE CICA TARIFF

As can be seen, there are many models available for tariffs, guides or *barèmes*. The purpose of this necessarily abbreviated and limited section is to demonstrate in a way relevant to the Scots system how, once it is accepted that awards are truly conventional rather than a matter of compensation, a degree of efficiency can be achieved. Appendix 5 shows various CICA tariff injuries allocated to certain fixed sums. It is constructed by dismantling the CICA tariff of 2001.[82] That tariff follows *in principle* the JSB and other systems by being arranged in such a way that it is intelligible to lawyers and lay users being set out by body part but is in its presentation divorced from issues such as permanence of disability. Naturally, it produces a very substantial list. However, there are only 25 different sums of money involved. Anyone from outside the legal system might think it better to focus on the 25 "bottom lines" instead of hundreds of descriptors (and descriptors which in the process will be adjudicated in fact by medical doctors). This reconstruction is limited to the first nine bands. There are two reasons for this restriction. First, smaller injuries and smaller awards are the very ones which create the worst cost–benefit ratios in that the work for a small claim can be much the same as a very large one and so the proportionate effect of transaction costs is at the highest level. Secondly, the present summary cause limit is £5,000 and so it is cases like these which are the most likely to be amenable to some form of fast tracking under the present system.

Of awards in the range selected, sexual abuse has been left out of account, as it might be thought different considerations apply. Physical abuse understandably appears in a criminal injuries scheme but is likely to be treated specially in a civil case rather than as a "menu item". Mental illness is left out, on account of the possibility that diagnosis might be more contentious among practitioners. These few items have had no

---

[81] *Note 80 above.* Curiously, this has a parallel on the State side in that the CICA report states that "Every year the scheme awards about £170m in compensation ... *This is more than all of the other European Union (EU) schemes put together*" (emphasis added): *RL*, p 3.
[82] As explained above, there is a new 2008 Scheme but it too is the same as the last one in having 25 bands and similar in having hundreds of injury descriptors.

overall effect on the picture revealed by the recasting of the lower part of the table.

The first thing which can be observed from the rearranged data in Appendix 4 is that some of the bands appear to be thinly populated. Why should this be? The answer may lie in consideration of toes, fingers and teeth. The tariff, in trying to be a shadow of the common law assessment system, is *calibrating* itself to reflect the bespoke approach. But, on the thesis of this book, that is a shadow of an illusion. Worse, at this level of small sums differentiating bands, it is workable only within a tariff: if the awards were bands, the overlap in bands would result in barely organised chaos. So there is an issue of diminishing returns in over-differentiation of a tariff of conventional awards. Applying that to the Appendix 4, Levels 2, 4, 6 and 8 could easily be merged with levels above or below. Without bringing to bear personal experience, it is perhaps the case that Level 9 does mark an increase in the general severity of the injuries. If so, for the sake of the consideration of the efficiency of the process, including the possibility of fast-tracking minor cases, then that level would be moved up (and out of any fast track). If, for the sake of caution, Level 8 is merged with 9, that leaves seven levels. Level 1 ought to be retained for the most minor injuries. If any similar structure were used for real common law cases, the CICA limitation on minimum discomfort would have to be removed as, so long as there is some harm, there must be some award. So that would mean Level 1 and the three merged bands: 2 and 3; 4 and 5; and 6 and 7 – a total of only four bands.

4. CONCLUSIONS

THE PRESENT SYSTEM OUGHT TO BE REFORMED

The present system of the assessment of non-pecuniary personal injury damages is fundamentally flawed in that it applies a sophisticated assessment process to what is a conventional award.[1]

The present system is defective in that awards are unnecessarily variable. Awards are variable horizontally among sheriffdoms. Awards are also variable vertically, depending on forum; thus, awards may differ depending upon whether the assessment is in the sheriff court, the Outer House, the Inner House, the Supreme Court or the jury court.[2]

The present system is defective because the background information required to come to a conventional figure is often incomplete.

Medical information is haphazard. The medical information may come from any source – there are no certificated authorised medical assessors. The medical information may be of any quality. To an extent, that may be related to source but, even assuming the best source, the information is obtained on a haphazard basis and is produced as the medical writer cares to produce it.

The legal information is limited. Published sources have improved dramatically but have never been comprehensive and they are declining a little because of improved extra-judicial settlement deriving from improved court procedures. Settlement figures are not comprehensively available.

---

[1] While other states may appear to do the same, this might be for reasons beyond those yielded in any limited survey. For example, in Germany there may indeed be more of a need for a bespoke approach to *Schmerzensgeld* because that award comprises redress (*Ausgleich*) with satisfaction (*Genugtuung*) (Decision BGH, 6 July 1955, translated by Y P Salmon, in W Van Gerven, *Cases, Materials and Text on National, Supranational and International Tort Law* (2000), p 754). Accordingly, the German award considers the degree of culpability of the wrongdoer, the financial position of the claimant and the economic circumstances of the wrongdoer.

[2] This does not result in a pure "x to the power y" problem because, assessments not being formally binding, it is possible for the sheriffs, sheriffs principal and Outer House judges to consider each others' awards in an attempt to reach consistency.

Court procedures allow actions simply to be dropped on settlement albeit that the Compensation Recovery Unit of the Government has detailed information derived from cases where the compensator is by law required to account to government. Compensation recovery, however, does not apply to non-pecuniary damages for pain and suffering. The insurance industry privately controls settlement data.

The present system is arguably defective because the only democratic input to the process is the occasional contribution of a randomly selected jury, itself not fully informed with data as to previous judicial or non-judicial settlements.

The present system is unnecessarily complex, to the extent of often involving many people carrying out the same task, and thus unnecessarily costly.

PATCHING UP THE PRESENT SYSTEM

On the coat-tails of JSB

At present it has been shown that the English JSB guidelines are in use in Scotland at judicial level and are fully incorporated into the relevant professional literature. In any event, in general, it is expected that awards will be similar on both sides of the border.[3] A full study of the entire system, canvassing the profession at all levels, would be needed to gauge the full extent of factual use, such as use in correspondence between solicitors and insurers. Certainly, use by Scots lawyers of the JSB is a commendably cheap way of going about obtaining some savings in time and cost as well as obtaining some degree of consistency. It is submitted, however, that, like any freeloading, borrowing the work of others without asking or giving anything in return is not something of which to be proud. There is no reason why an independent legal system operating in a devolved political system should use anything other than

---

[3] See, eg, *Duthie* v *Macfish Ltd* 2001 SLT 833: "It is, in my view, appropriate for me to take note of the decision of the Court of Appeal in *Heil* [v *Rankin* [2000] 2 WLR 1173]. In doing so, I am not undertaking the task undertaken by the Court of Appeal of reviewing the general level of awards (at [2000] 2 WLR at 1200C, para 82). I am simply having regard to what is now the current level of awards in England. It has been clear since *Allan* v *Scott* [1972 SC 59; 1972 SLT 45] that it is appropriate to do that. I am not bound by *Heil*, but I would in my view be going against the spirit of *Allan* v *Scott*, by which I am bound, if I were to ignore it" (per Lord Macfadyen at para 28). However, when faced with a new kind of injury to value – a lengthy period of child abuse – a Scottish court declined to look at Irish awards: *J* v *Fife Council* 2007 SLT 85 at 92.

its own figures.[4] The very considerable divergence in awards in fatal cases proves that the two nations may hold very different views as to what a conventional award should be: the English have a low (by comparison) fixed conventional figure and the Scots a (usually) high bespoke figure.

Joining JSB

There is a Scottish Judicial Studies Committee. It dates back only to 1997, has only a small staff and comprises, among others, very experienced members of the judiciary. With the resources at its disposal it carries out a huge range of work, including the training of new sheriffs and updating the manual from which jury charges in serious criminal cases are derived. It is to take charge of training law justices.[5] Against that background of mission-critical work and restricted resources, it would be stretched indeed to prepare a new set of guidelines of its own. The United Kingdom Judicial Studies Council is a forum in which the judicial training institutions for England and Wales (the Judicial Studies Board), Scotland and Northern Ireland meet and exchange information about a wide variety of matters of mutual interest, including the possibility of common training in the future.[6] It is not impossible that that body could be at least a "clearing house" sponsor, validator or liaison body for a common set of guidelines derived from the JSB. There would still be a cost saving so far as administration is concerned. It would keep Scots and English awards close if that is still thought to be desirable (outside of fatal cases where it is not thought desirable).

Mac–JSB

However, it may be that the time has come for Scotland to set its own figures reflecting its own culture on what ought to be paid and if that means more money to the Scottish JSB then so be it.[7] When Australia reviewed its system it was noted that awards varied considerably across the various Australian states.[8] There was the same issue of smaller

---

[4] An exception to that point would be if there were homogenous European figures but, as has been demonstrated, none exists.
[5] Annual Report, March 2007.
[6] JSB Annual Report, 2006–2007, p 8.
[7] On the figures available from ONS, it did not appear that Scots valuations were radically different from those of the rest of the Great Britain in relation to the 18-month whiplash case: ONS, p 126. (See Appendix 5.)
[8] Panel of Eminent Persons, *Review of the Law of Negligence Final Report*, October 2002 (Ipp Report), para 13.8.

claims costing considerably more than higher-value claims.[9] The review recommended an Australian version of the English JSB.[10]

It is possible that if civil jury trial is to remain and there is not to be a tariff, a *Scots* JSB guide could be used to give guidance to juries. We know from Lord Hope's speech in a House of Lords case that when he was Chair of the Rules Council there was debate about giving guidance in fatal cases which did not provide any easy answer.[11] A Scots JSB might provide a solution. It would in any event improve the process of ordinary claims.

DEMOCRATIC INTERVENTION: A PAIN AND SUFFERING DAMAGES COMMISSION OR COMMISSIONER

Even with the various possible JSB solutions, many of the problems identified above remain. There remains a range of awards rather than a single figure capable of de-skilled administrative handling. The figures are not mandatory and so time cost and expense may still be incurred as set out above and exemplified in the appendices. There is still a democratic gap in that the conventional figures do not have the consent of the governed. The cases would be decided against a variable background of medical information and out-of-court work would still be affected by the secret expert systems of the insurance industry.

Beyond simply patching the present system, it would be possible to take a reforming step by introducing a democratic element. That alone would not reduce cost much but would establish guidelines as the primary focus of the exercise. So, as a further and improved variant of the "patched-up" model, the conventional levels utilised by the courts could be set by some kind of body – a Pain and Suffering Damages Commission or Commissioner.[12] As a result of the publication of the Gill Report, no suggestions are made here as to how such a body would be composed, how often it ought to meet or conduct its business. It could

---

[9] Ipp Report, para 13.5.
[10] *Ibid*, paras 13.25–13.26.
[11] *Girvan* v *Inverness Farmers Dairy* 1998 SC (HL) 1 at 21.
[12] This section mirrors a proposal made by the present author in response to the Scottish Law Commission Discussion Paper on fatal cases. That response suggested a Grief Damages Commission. It was not taken forward after consultation. Obviously, if such ever existed, it could simply take over the task of pain and suffering damages – or vice versa.

be a committee of the "great and good" or it could be a part-time commissioner with a secretary to gather information and if required to commission research. That would depend upon the scope of the project. As the suggestions in this book all fall within the court process, then as there is the possibility of a Civil Justice Council for Scotland being established following on the Gill Report;[13] the proposed Commission or Commissioner could easily be established under the auspices of the proposed Gill Report body. The "Gill" body would have power to commission research which would be the key to ensuring that any tariff was (and remained) appropriate.

Assuming that there was a desire to establish a tariff, initial levels could be set on the basis of the English JSB, although it might be thought better to have a fresh start by first commissioning a statistical study discovering what ordinary people really think, such as was obtained by the English Law Commission.[14] Relevantly for this book which considers cost, the questionnaires for that English Law Commission study first gave the injury scenario, asking for an award level, and then the interviewee was informed that the cost of the compensation would be spread – perhaps resulting in increased insurance premiums. They were then asked whether, knowing that, they would alter their view,[15] and by how much in what direction.[16] Some 80 per cent of the Great Britain respondents and 80 per cent of the Scots respondents would not alter their view.[17] Some of the inherent problems of democracy are revealed by the ONS figures. The case most relevant to this book is that of a 34-year-old woman who suffers whiplash-type injury in a road traffic accident, has some pain immediately but is fully recovered in 18 months but with some continuing lack of confidence.[18] The ONS figures in Appendix 5 originate in 1998; the CICA figures, included here for a recasting exercise in Appendix 4, derive from 2001. It will be seen that whiplash over 13 weeks is a Level 6 award at £2,500. It has been noted that there is the possibility that the only democratic element available at present, the jury, sometimes does award about twice a judicial figure and in fact juries are not really allowed to do more than that. Thus, Case

---

[13] Gill Report, Chapter 1, paras 81–82; Chapter 15.
[14] ONS.
[15] *Ibid*, p 180.
[16] *Ibid*, p 181.
[17] *Ibid*, p 127.
[18] *Ibid*, p 179. See Appendix 5 for the full text of this scenario which is called "Case D" in the report.

D might in a court around 1998 have come in at £2,500 or £5,000.[19] Insurance companies would therefore be alarmed at the democratic data which shows that in Great Britain 54 per cent of the population sampled would have awarded more than that and, in Scotland, 56 per cent. More alarming would be the 15 per cent in GB and the 15 per cent in Scotland who would have made an award over £20,000, 10 per cent of the GB total awarding in excess of £40,000! Another way of looking at the numbers, taking into account the low awards, is that only about 12 per cent of the views of the Scots consulted would be considered accurate under the present system. Is such data collection worthwhile? It is submitted that it is, both as a cross-check on previous practice which has been to collect the haphazard and also as validation. It is submitted it is uncontroversial to say that most citizens will not be surprised to learn that some of their fellows hold extreme views – some jurors will be National Front racists, believe in Jedi Knights, play with toy cars or be undetected criminals,[20] just like the population as a whole. So it might not be at all controversial to exclude the views of the 10 per cent of citizens who would have awarded a "stingy" £100 maximum and those who would have awarded a "generous" over £40,000. Statisticians can do better than this and with a very much bigger sample their science would allow, for example, for the exclusion of certain wholly deviant responses and better focus.

Accordingly, data collection would be a very valuable first step. Statistical analysis of a bigger sample of a wider range of cases might well throw up some clear way-points, but it seems probable that decisions would have to be taken to establish clear bands. It would be possible and perhaps desirable to have a second round of data collection and statistical analysis along the lines of "regardless of your views the last time ... what do you think of this chart?".

The present deliberately uninformed occasional group of lay people who get a restricted say (jurors) are of course not a representative sample of the Scots population – they are too small a group in total and there are rules excluding Scots from jury service.

Another variant would be to collect the data based on questions derived from JSB using the exercise to see whether, and to what extent, JSB would require attenuation.

---

[19] If considered seriously disabling – not permanent – then the award is a Band 10 worth £5,500 which, doubled by a jury, would be £11,000: 24 per cent of GB respondents would have awarded over £10,000 and 22 per cent of Scots.

[20] These are to illustrate the diversity of the population and it is not being suggested that they are *eiusdem generis*.

REVOLUTION:
THE IRISH QUESTION

Similarly, some solution along the lines of the PIAB might be considered. Again, it must be emphasised that it is the system that is being discussed and not the level of awards. The Irish *Book of Quantum* is publicly available and under democratic control.[21] The Irish PIAB scheme could be monitored to see if it might be adapted for Scotland. It has been reported that "the Irish High Court has seen a reduction in personal injury claims lodged from 15,500 in 2004 to 404 as of September 2005".[22] Again, on a positive note, it is reported, PIAB says that the cost of its process is 10 per cent of every award. This contrasts with figures released by the Motor Insurance Advisory Board which stated that, in 2004, 46 per cent of every award payment went on litigation costs.[23] The Irish High Court saw a reduction in personal injury claims lodged from 15,500 in 2004 to 404 as of September 2005.[24] So perhaps there are other ways. It is impossible to say whether there is any need at all for a PIAB in Scotland without knowing whether there is an unmet need by claimants to be able to claim in the first place and without knowing whether the present system is failing claimants and respondents in processing claims which do not fall within the new court procedures. If the Court of Session reforms continue to prove to be successful[25] then the idea of replacing an effective system for medium- to high-value cases would need to be very persuasive indeed. Some have argued that state systems have limitations, and such arguments undoubtedly have force.[26] There has already been vehement comment arguing that Scotland should

---

[21] In relation to "Case D" discussed above, it may be noted that the Irish *Book of Quantum* has, for whiplash, "Substantially recovered within 24 months €11,500 [£9,245] to €17,400 [£13,989]" (illustrative currency conversions as at 16/4/2008).

[22] E Roberts, "Claims before the Personal Injuries Assessment Board Newsletter"; A & L Goodbody (December 2005): http://www.algoodbody.ie/ezinelitigation/article.asp?9+56 (accessed 8/10/09).

[23] *Ibid.*

[24] *Ibid.*

[25] "The Coulsfield rules ... have been outstandingly successful in encouraging realistic settlements and in removing much of the intrinsic delay of the old procedure. The average time between raising and settlement in my firm's cases is now less than six months": G Garrett, "A Breach of Protocol" 2008 (Feb) JLSS 14 at 14. They are being adapted and introduced into the sheriff court: Act of Sederunt (Ordinary Cause Rules Amendment) (Personal Injuries Actions) 2009 (SSI 2009/285).

[26] See generally Atiyah, *Lottery*, Chapter 8: "What can we do about it?".

not "copy the Irish".[27] That comment refers to criticism in the Irish Press and concludes that the apparent cost savings are as a result of diverting costs to claimants who end up using solicitors at their own expense in 90 per cent of cases.[28] Lawyers and citizens are well aware of the difficulties resulting from the removal of alimentary claims from the courts by the creation of the Child Support Agency. That said, the PIAB itself is worthy of close monitoring. It may be that such systems work better in smaller homogenous states, such as Eire and New Zealand.[29] The present system is to a large extent in the private sector[30] and to establish a state body would be to divert more activity to the public sector.[31]

These conclusions – against a revolution – are consonant with the Gill Report. It expressly does not recommend a non-court system.[32] The Gill Report also recognises the fundamental point identified above – that the PIAB was a response to a small insurance pool.[33] As explained above, that is not (yet) the situation in Scotland, although it must be appreciated that if that ever happened, perhaps as a result of independence, more urgent consideration of the PIAB might be required.[34] Nonetheless, the mission of this book is quite different and more narrow than the issues confronting the Gill Review. The interest for this thesis is the success or otherwise of the non-practitioner use of the *Book of Quantum* in assessing non-pecuniary damages. So the Gill Report conclusion that it should be monitored before consideration be given to use of it is valuable.[35] It would, however, be possible to reject a full PIAB but adopt or learn lessons from the use of the *Book of Quantum*.

---

[27] Garrett, *Protocol*, p 16.
[28] *Ibid*.
[29] Cane, *Accidents*, pp 467–488.
[30] The courts are public, although they do charge for many services.
[31] See, generally, R Marsh and F Zuleeg, *The Scottish Public Sector: Does Size Matter?* (September 2006) Hume Occasional Paper no 69.
[32] Gill Report, Chapter 4, para 151.
[33] *Ibid*, Chapter 4, para 152.
[34] Not because of the political change but because of the possibility of fracturing the insurance pool. Australia faced similar problems to Eire in 2002, requiring a complete examination of tort law there with subsequent legislative intervention: Panel of Eminent Persons, *Review of the Law of Negligence Final Report*, October 2002 (Ipp Report).
[35] Gill Report, Chapter 4, para 152. This footnote records the fact that a study is under way, funded by the Irish Research Council for Humanities and Social Sciences and being conducted at University College Dublin School of Law by J Ilan and C Scott.

MULTI-TRACK HYBRID: A PARTIAL DEMOCRATIC "MEDICALISED" TARIFF

A multi-track hybrid tariff-based model

Assume, as seems wise in the present early years of the PIAB, that "Irish" reform is not favoured and, in view of the Gill Report, entirely unlikely. Assume too that patching up seems like a lot of effort for little or no return. Then, it is submitted that many desirable aims can be achieved by some partially revolutionary change but operating within the existing judicial system. The basic model is as follows.

High-value cases are likely to cost money on grounds of disputed liability or contributory negligence or complex pecuniary damages. So, absent a completely publicly administered system, the cost of assessment of non-pecuniary damage is at least shared in the overall cost. Smaller cases cost the most proportionally and if removed from the system give higher gains. Political/democratic agreement is more likely to be achieved around basic bodily injury cases as opposed to child abuse or paraplegia. Basic injuries are more amenable to medical standardisation. Standardised medical outcomes are more amenable to the allocation of money to the disability/permanence of any standardised medical output. A publicly approved, medically validated tariff emerges from the foregoing. At a publicly acceptable, judicially practicable, level, cases can be diverted into an administrative track within the umbrella of the court system.

Based on the arguments in the paper and this model, the following points require some elaboration. It is believed that there is nothing in this court-located model which conflicts with the general approach of the Gill Report; rather, the creation of, for example, a Central Personal Injury Court would provide a foundation for evolution.

Medicalisation

Medicalisation – passing issues to the medical profession to adjudicate – is a form of de-lawyering. It is clearly not de-skilling. Medical time may be as costly as legal time. The benefit here is to have less and better medical involvement and as a result of issues of disability/permanence and dysfunction dealt with by professionals who understand it, at the same time removing it from those who do not. If some new Scottish structure were to be erected, it might be better to look forward and to Europe and consider reform of the medical information system – these are the true facts upon which the system works. So, instead of moving straightaway to a JSB-type table based on previous judicial history (itself simply the result of traditional growth), a more scientific *barème* model, which would start from medical diagnoses and move towards points, could be developed. Such tables can build in the ideas of whether something heals immediately or has consequence. It can be built around what doctors can or cannot say rather than trying to see if the doctor can speak to a "legal category". That would require a "conversation" with initial input probably from the medical Royal Colleges. The benefit for the medical profession is that it would find it much easier to process the many demands for reports. Pro forma reports[36] would cut down administrative cost and waste in the NHS which has to process this work, albeit often now charging out full economic cost so that the NHS budget is not affected. (Although it is still a cost and a substantial one which is fed back to premium payers and taxpayers.) It would eliminate from the present process the £150 medical report from the local GP which, after four reminders and 5 months of waiting, advises that "This patient had an accident and is still quite poorly". Indeed, while this book has been in preparation the Department for Constitutional Affairs in England and Wales has, through work with stakeholders, developed a standard medical template "intended to point medical experts to the issues that they need to cover in their report".[37]

One issue which would have to be addressed is whether an actual value would be assigned or whether, as with the European model, conditions are assigned a percentage reduction from the total. Insurers and statisticians would prefer this model as it keeps payments broadly within predictable limits and makes the scheme more easy to manage. Claimants and judges might feel it is just too restrictive. Politicians could be found, as usual, on both sides. Of course, the world outside of the traditional legal profession (including the medical profession) has been familiar with this kind of system for over a century through Workmen's Compensation whereby today in Scotland disability is assessed and compensated on a percentage basis.[38] Even the ordinary common law has a model known only to personal injury specialists and that is in relation to Vibration-Induced White Finger or Reynaud's phenomenon or Hand–Arm Vibration

---

[36] For a pro forma medical report, see that of the PIAB which can be found in the following section: http://www.injuriesboard.ie/eng/Forms_and_Publications/ (accessed 8/10/09).

[37] DCA-CP, para 64 and Appendix 6. That scheme is still having doctors work in service of the guidelines rather than preparing guidelines based around what can be said by experts as to disability/disadvantage and the duration, or likely duration, thereof.

[38] Presently the main benefit is Industrial Injuries Disablement Benefit: Social Security Contributions and Benefit Act 1992.

Syndrome. Here the practice is to use one or both of the well-known medical scales to support the disability level claimed.[39]

The CICA restructuring offered in Appendix 4 suggests that, at the lower end at least, some simple expeditious system could be devised, utilising medically certified disability. The discussion of the statistical approach above also suggests that, with thought and work, a limited exercise could be conducted to cross-check quantification.

It would not be difficult to arrange for medical general practitioners to complete a simple form placing the injuries in one of the four bands. A separate system of medical appeals could exist whereby if the pursuer's medical form was disputed by service of a counter-form, a court-appointed medical person would decide. A "special cause shown" formula very familiar in civil procedure could be used to allow for some unforeseen types of cases to be diverted back to court, the rules being modified in light of experience. The quantum is then fixed and that aspect of a claim can be handled by the sheriff clerk. Such a system would facilitate the use of the voluntary pre-action protocol. It would enhance the compulsory protocol envisaged by the Gill Report. It would put an end to litigation which should never have been forced on the pursuer (or the public purse) by an insurer's robot.

A partial tariff

Following the CICA tariff reform, we could move to adopting some form of banding approach to reduce cost and delay, essentially removing the matter from judicial consideration and switching it to democratic review. As the Scottish Law Commission appreciated in its discussion of fatal cases, some of the gains of a tariff may be lost for each element of flexibility which is introduced.[40] However, the CICA system shows that it is possible to build in a review procedure and that judicial review is available should the basic running of the system go awry. It is worth emphasising

---

[39] Fully discussed in R Conway, *Personal Injury Practice in the Sheriff Court* (W Green, 2nd edn, 2003), pp 253 *et seq*. This title includes practical guidance on how to run such a case with reference to the Stockholm and Taylor-Pelmear scales. For illustrations in Scots practice, see *Smith* v *Shaw & McInnes Ltd*, OH, Lord McEwan, 24 April 2001; *Agnew* v *Scott Lithgow*, IH, 1 April 2003, and earlier (OH) 5 April 2002; *Burke* v *Glasgow City Council* [2005] CSOH 155. A detailed examination of the two scales, compared and contrasted (and with an element of medical dispute) can be found in *Deans* v *George Newberry Coachbuilders*, Airdrie Sheriff Court, 13 September 2005. See also *Conway* v *Hytec Hydraulic Engineering Ltd*, Sh Bicket, Hamilton, 23 March 2007.
[40] SLC, *Wrongful Death*, para 3.65.

that the reduction of cost and delay is not at all to enhance the profits of insurance companies – damages are paid from premiums, not profits. The solace of solatium is more effective if it comes quickly after the injury, all the sooner to pacify rancour. The sooner the claim is concluded, the sooner some individuals recover. In the course of preparation of this book the Department for Constitutional Affairs in England and Wales has consulted on whether an assessment tool should be developed for general damages for pain and suffering because these would "increase transparency and reduce delay and cost" and could be either "a computerised tool or a more sophisticated form of JSB guidelines, with narrower bands for injuries".[41]

On the basis of the restructuring offered for the 2001 CICA tariff, it is submitted that, at a sufficiently low level, very few bands are in fact required but it could be prudent to utilise the statistical method discussed above.

The tariff and administration

To gain the full benefit of a tariff, the tariff cases need to go out of the ordinary legal process, although not necessarily outside of the control of the court. Under a tariff system, professional time will have been spent by the medical profession in assessing the hurt, and if the idea of some commission to fix awards is taken up, there is the annual professional work in fixing the tariff. To gain from these costs there should be as little cost in applying the tariff as is possible. Liability issues often become easier once the cost of admitting liability is settled. It is worth looking at some actual recent changes in the judicial system. First, a "justice gap" was removed, taking personal injury small claims cases back into the mainstream. Secondly, and most importantly for this book, the summary cause limit was taken up to £5,000 at the same time as the privative jurisdiction of the sheriff court. While this has been subject to informed criticism,[42] to have actions for a few thousand pounds in the Court of Session has always seemed, to the present writer at least, something of a "Rolls Royce service for a bicycle". Happily, it may soon disappear under the proposals in the Gill Report.[43] However, the point is this: now that more personal injury cases might be expected in the sheriff summary court, it might make

---

[41] DCA-CP, para 84.
[42] Conway, *Colossus*, p 16.
[43] Gill Report, Chapter 4, para 123, sending cases up to £150,000 to the sheriff court. Also at vol 1, p ii and Chapter 2, para 30.

sense to have a statutory table of quantum for cases up to that limit of £5,000. This would be something which could be used perhaps by sheriff clerks in the preliminary process to help focus issues – especially where parties might be unrepresented and most certainly would allow sheriffs to expedite some causes. The parallel with such a solution can be seen from the history of sheriff court reform where we have seen in the past "quickie" divorces and small estates executries being run using simple forms and the offices and efforts of the sheriff clerk. Such a modest start would be consonant with the Gill Report which understandably utilises this relatively new and un-researched £5,000 limit as the threshold for the work of the proposed new district judge operating a new simplified procedure.[44] A sub-£5,000 tariff would provide the district judge, who might not be a personal injury specialist, with a useful tool to manage the case at an early stage simply by determining within which of maybe five bands the parties consider the hurt falls. A standardised medical report would facilitate this exercise.

Alternatively, taking account of the modest range of injuries which would fall within a £5,000 limit, it might be argued that a figure of £10,000 would be a better use of a tariff. This figure comes from the basic limit of the present Law Society of Scotland voluntary pre-action protocol scheme. This system is a kind of informal version of the Woolf reforms, allowing insurers in Scotland to run their cases in a way similar to the way in which their cases are run in England.[45] The attraction of setting the limit at this level is that it would benefit insurers and keep costs down and it might also benefit claimants' lawyers because under the scheme there are percentage fees not related directly to the time spent on the case. Provided that the overall level of payout is kept the same, claimants and their lawyers would not lose and premium payers would gain. The Gill Report supports the voluntary protocol and would extend it and make it compulsory,[46] so indeed this might be a good place to introduce a restricted partial tariff, with parties being obliged at an early stage to indicate the particular tariff point.

So either a summary cause level tariff or a voluntary protocol tariff would provide a system of value in its own right and a test to see whether

---

[44] Gill Report, Chapter 2, para 37.
[45] However, one leading firm has discovered that the protocol is much less efficient in producing settlement than the improved Court of Session procedures, themselves inspired by the English Woolf reforms: Garrett, *Protocol*.
[46] Gill Report, Chapter 8, paras 33–36. Indeed it suggests developing a new protocol for clinical negligence: para 35.

it might be extended higher up the range of value. If it works, and with the benefit of experience, it could be gradually extended up the range of value until it encounters diminishing returns, whether by cost or ever more frequent attempt to exit administration and to return to full judicial control.

APPENDICES

APPENDIX 1
COURT-DISPUTED NON-PECUNIARY LOSS (LOW VALUE)

A typical dispute over non-pecuniary loss of a small amount. This one has been selected because it has been very well handled by the parties' lawyers and the judgment, on appeal, is exemplary. It is thus intended to reflect "how it is done properly" under the present system.

Symington v *Milne*, Edinburgh, 4 May 2007.

1. This appeal arises following proof in an action of damages for personal injuries. The action was not defended on the merits; the medical evidence was in substance agreed and the only witness to give evidence was the pursuer.

2. The pursuer's accident took place on 23 June 2004. The Sheriff made the following findings in fact consequent upon the proof: "(3) That as a result of said accident the pursuer sustained muscular damage to her neck. (4) That the pursuer was seen at the Royal Infirmary Edinburgh immediately following said accident where she was examined and discharged with painkillers. (5) Thereafter the pursuer spent four days in bed as a result of pain suffered by her. (6) Thereafter the pursuer sustained neck pain which was treated by a combination of analgesics and physiotherapy until about the end of the year. (7) That during said time the pursuer was not able to carry out her household duties to the full and was inhibited from playing in any sort of boisterous way her with twin sons aged four. (8) That for said four days the household duties in the pursuer's house was carried out by her partner. (9) That between the time of the accident and about October 2004 the pursuer's mother came regularly to the pursuer's home to do household work to help her. (10) By the end of 2004 the pursuer

had to all intents and purposes recovered from the pain and injury caused by said accident".

3. On the basis of these findings, and in light of a number of decided cases cited to him by both parties the sheriff concluded that the appropriate figure for solatium was £1,250.00. He further awarded the pursuer £250.00 in respect of services received by her from her mother and partner. The appeal proceeds on two grounds. The first of these is that in making finding-in-fact 10 the sheriff placed an incomplete or erroneous interpretation on an agreed medical report prepared by Professor A H R Simpson on 3 May 2005. It was contended that a proper reading of that report would lead to an interpretation that the pursuer continued to suffer symptoms beyond the end of 2004. In submissions the solicitor for the pursuer and appellant contended that finding-in-fact 10 should be altered to reflect the fact that the pursuer had minor neck tenderness and restricted neck movement in 2005 and required physiotherapy in October and November 2005 to relieve the residual symptoms caused by the injury sustained by the accident. In the light of that the sum awarded by way of solatium fell to be revised. The second, and alternative, ground of appeal is that even if no such amendment to finding-in-fact 10 is to be made an award of £1,250.00 by way of solatium was nevertheless unreasonable.

4. The solicitor for the pursuer and appellant accepted the reluctance of an appellate court to interfere with factual findings made by a court of first instance. However he contended that there was sufficient reason to interfere with finding-in-fact 10 made by the sheriff. The report by Professor Simpson, which had been agreed by parties as true and accurate with the exception of one sentence relating to prognosis, set out that the pursuer had severe neck pain for approximately one month and that thereafter the pain gradually subsided over the follow six months. At the time of his examination in May 2005 Professor Simpson noted that the pursuer had minimal symptoms which were not intrusive in her life in any way but she did have "a minimal restriction of movement of her neck". That in itself did not support a finding of complete recovery by the end of 2004; there was, however, further support for the view that the pursuer's symptoms persisted longer in the form of a report from BUPA indicating that she had received physiotherapy

between October and November 2005, and the pursuer herself had given evidence to the effect that this treatment was sought because of the "ongoing neck injury", on the advice of Professor Simpson (see Notes pages 16 to 17). This evidence, it was contented, had not been challenged in cross-examination.

5. I am not persuaded that the sheriff's conclusions unfairly reflect the terms of Professor Simpson's report. The overall impression, conveyed both by the findings and by what is recorded by Professor Simpson as having been related to him by the pursuer, is that recovery was complete in about seven months following the accident. This follows from the pursuer's statement that pain was severe for approximately one month and that it gradually subsided over the following six. That timescale would take one slightly beyond the end of 2004. Finding-in-fact 10 might be more accurately have reflected Professor Simpson's report if it had stated that by early 2005 the pursuer had to all intents and purposes recovered but I doubt whether that justifies interference. In any event finding-in-fact 6 which sets out that the pain "was treated by a combination of analgesics and physiotherapies until about the end of the year" is a finding which could not be seriously questioned.

6. As to the evidence of physiotherapy in 2005 the difficulty is that the sheriff observed in a short paragraph on page 4 of his Note that "the further physiotherapy received by the pursuer is not in evidence related to injuries caused to her by the accident". I find it slightly difficult to know what to make of that. It is certainly the case that the pursuer gave evidence to the effect that this physiotherapy was given on the advice of Professor Simpson and was related to the neck injury. Whilst the pursuer was asked in cross-examination (see Notes page 22) whether that physiotherapy was necessitated by a pre-existing problem of sciatica, no evidence was led on behalf of the defender to that effect. That would tend to support the submissions made on the pursuer's behalf, but it may well be that the sheriff simply found the pursuer's evidence unconvincing in the light of Professor Simpson's report which indicated a recovery around the end of 2004. This whole area of evidence is rendered even more opaque by the terms of the joint minute of admissions in terms of which Professor Simpson's report was accepted as true and accurate with exception of the sentence

which reads "I consider that she may benefit from a further course of physiotherapy to help her regain full movement (maximum of six sessions)". The implication of that must be that the suggestion that the pursuer required physiotherapy in 2005 for injuries caused in the accident was the subject of challenge. The position is not assisted by the fact that the agreement in relation to the BUPA report states that it is to be "treated as a true and accurate copy of the pursuer's discharge form". That does not seem to me to amount to more than an agreement that the pursuer received physiotherapy in the autumn of 2005. Overall the picture presented is not one in which I could with confidence reach the conclusion that the evidence presented to me on the printed page justifies interference with the sheriff's conclusion that it was not proved that the physiotherapy in the autumn of 2005 related to the injury sustained in the accident.

7. I accordingly turn to the second ground of appeal which relates to the amount awarded by way of solatium for the pursuer's injuries. In this respect her solicitor accepted that this was a matter in which an appellate court would not interfere with the discretion exercised at first instance "unless the sum awarded is out of all proportion to what the court thinks should have been awarded": (see Macphail, *Sheriff Court Practice* (3rd edn), para 18 116 and the authorities cited therein). Accepting that the pursuer sustained muscular damage to her neck which resulted in four days in bed followed by neck pain which required analgesics for a further six months; inability to carry out household duties or play with her twin sons and a setback in returning to work he nevertheless contended that the figure of £1,250.00 awarded was wholly unreasonable. In reviewing a number of reported decisions on quantum on similar cases the pursuer's solicitor started with a decision of my own in *Armstrong* v *Brake Brothers Ltd* 2003 SLT 58 in which I indicated that a stiff neck resulting from whiplash injuries could be a painful and debilitating condition which justified an award of solatium of £350.00 even when it lasted only for a matter of a few days. In *Pugh* v *Scott* (2002 Rep LR 112) Sheriff Mackie in this court awarded £2,500.00 by way of solatium to a 32-year-old pursuer who suffered severe pain for the first four weeks after the accident but was not off work, did not require physiotherapy and whose symptoms had fully resolved in about five months following the accident. That

award, it was suggested, would with the effect of inflation be the equivalent of about £2,800.00 now. In *Monaghan* v *Sim* (Sheriff Baird, Glasgow Sheriff Court, 29 September 2005) an award of £3,000.00 was made. The pursuer there had visited his GP on five occasions and physiotherapist on four occasions. He required to take painkillers for two months and suffered pain and discomfort for six months following which he made a full recovery. Lastly, in *Morris* v *Sutherland* (Sheriff Dunbar, Dunfermline Sheriff Court, 3 August 2006, unreported) £2,750.00 was awarded to a pursuer who sustained injuries resulting in pain in his back and hip which lasted for about five months. These decisions it was contended all pointed to solatium for a whiplash injury which resulted in six months or so of suffering to be of the order of £2,500.00 to £3,000.00. On the basis that this was at least twice that awarded by the sheriff it would be appropriate to intervene.

8. In reply on this issue the solicitors for the defenders submitted that the sheriff's award fell within a proper and reasonable bracket. On any view it was not so low as to be wholly unreasonable. The figure given in the guidelines for the assessment of general damages in personal injury cases compiled by the Judicial Studies Board in England (7th edn, 2004) gave a range of £750.00 to £2,500.00 for minor soft tissue and whiplash injuries where the symptoms were moderate and full recovery took place within a few weeks and a year. On the basis that the pursuer recovered in six months, £1,250.00 would be reasonable if the award was one of general damages. In *Quinn* v *Bowie* 1987 SLT 575 the pursuer sustained a whiplash injury which required him to be fitted with a collar. The pain in the middle of his back took two to three months to pass off and he had continuing discomfort for a total period of around eight months. The award was £700.00 which would be approximately £1,400.00 now. Reference was made *to D (a child)* v *Bernard Shenton Ltd* Current Law Cases (2003) 1 QR 15 in which the brief note indicates that by way of general damages £1,750.00 was awarded to a 15-year-old male for symptoms of whiplash injury which took 12 months to resolve. That would now be worth slightly more than £2,000.00. £1,000.00 was awarded in *Andrews* v *Hill* (Romford County Court, 21 May 2004, unreported) for whiplash injuries in which the prognosis was a recovery within seven to ten months of the accident. Reverting to Scottish cases,

reliance was placed on *Fairley* v *Thomson*, a decision of Sheriff Allan in this court on 2 September 2004. In that case it was noted that the pursuer "suffered a fair degree of discomfort; was unable to work for a period of five days but the pain in the neck and back as a result of normal day to day activities had cleared up in a period of approximately six weeks". It was further noted that the pursuer was unable to undertake a physical training regime which he was accustomed to and that "the whole situation" might take a number of months or even up to two years to be completely resolved. The award therein was £1,700.00. £2,250.00 was awarded by Sheriff K M Stewart in *Ferguson* v *City Refrigeration Holdings (UK) Ltd* 2005 Rep LR 117. In that case the sheriff had observed that although the pursuer had regarded himself as being fully recovered from his injuries some seven months after the accident he still had some discomfort. It was suggested that this was a case where the symptoms were of a much longer duration than the present. Lastly, in *Chambers* v *Forbes* (Sheriff Miller, Ayr Sheriff Court, 12 August 2005, unreported) an award of £2,500.00 was considered appropriate in a case where the pursuer's symptoms lasted for a year.

9. There are two general comments which I wish to make before turning to my conclusions in relation to these submissions. The first is that, whilst the older cases serve as some guide, I am inclined to the view that awards for whiplash injuries may be proportionally higher than they were some years ago. This increase reflects a greater awareness of the debilitating effect of injuries of this type which, as I observed in *Armstrong* v *Brake Brothers*, can be of a most painful nature. Secondly, whilst there is no question that the approach to valuing solatium for soft tissue injuries should take into account primarily the severity of those injuries for the purposes at arriving at a position on the scale of appropriate awards, it is also necessary to take into account elements of subjectivity which arise in every case. The pursuer here was a lady who had two boisterous children to care for. It is appropriate to distinguish that from the case, for example, of a 15-year-old as in *D* v *Bernard Shenton*, although the injuries themselves may not be dissimilar. Most cases involve their own particular features, for example, in *Fairley* v *Thomson* the pursuer was very active and the injury resulted in restriction of his physical training regime.

10. Nevertheless it is important that there should be a degree of consistency in awards for injuries of a similar nature and in this respect it is very difficult to reconcile the award made by the Sheriff here with that in *Pugh* v *Scott*. In both cases the pursuer was in his/her 30s. The pursuer in *Pugh* was not off work. Whilst he was restricted in what he could do, he had fully recovered after a period of about five months. About the most that could be said to justify the higher award in that case was that the injuries restricted his preparations for Christmas. Although the award made in *Pugh* does strike me as being on the high side – indeed it was at the top end of the scale suggested by the pursuer's solicitor – I do not consider that it was inconsistent with other cases. *Ferguson* v *City Refrigeration Holdings* was I consider a case very similar to the present. The period of recovery was almost exactly the same. There was only one attendance for medical treatment. Whilst the sheriff accepted that at the date of the proof the pursuer still had "an occasional twinge in the shoulder" that does not seem to me to be far removed from the finding in the present case that the pursuer has "to all intents and purposes" recovered.

11. The sheriff in the present case gives no particular reason for determining the figure of £1,250.00 to be appropriate, nor does he compare the circumstances with those of any of the cases cited to him. In my view an appropriate award of solatium would have been £2,250.00 which is substantially higher than that awarded and such, I consider, as to justify interference.

12. In all these circumstances I shall vary the interlocutor of 13 October by increasing the sum awarded by £1,000.00. As requested, I have reserved all questions of expenses.

APPENDIX 2

COURT-DISPUTED NON-PECUNIARY DAMAGES (MEDIUM VALUE) (JSB USE) (OTHER DISPUTED ISSUES)

This extract shows the traditional approach and the use of the JSB. It will be clear from the gaps in the paragraph numbering that the non-pecuniary part of this case was only a small part of a larger case. It involves much more varied and serious injury than the previous case.

Munnoch v *Tay-Forth Foundries Ltd* [2007] CSOH 159
(Lord Kinclaven)

Introduction

[1] This is a reparation action in which the pursuer seeks damages for personal injuries sustained in an accident at work on 27 November 2003.

[2] The pursuer is a metal dresser to trade. He was working on a platform at the defenders' foundry premises when he fell backwards about 10 feet to the ground and injured his back. He was 39 years of age at the time.

[3] Liability is admitted. The amended sum sued for is £250,000.

[4] The matter came before me by way of proof restricted to quantum of damages.

[...]

The background

[9] The pursuer was born on 1 June 1964 and lives with his partner in Stenhousemuir, Larbert.

[10] As a result of the accident, he suffered a burst fracture of the 12th thoracic vertebra and injured his back. He was in hospital for about four weeks and he continues to suffer as a result of the accident.

[11] The averments of loss are in Article 5 of Condescendence.

[12] In Article 5 the pursuer claims damages under the following heads:

(i) solatium for pain and suffering (past and future);
(ii) loss of earnings (past and future);
(iii) disadvantage on the labour market;
(iv) past services under section 8 of the Administration of Justice Act 1982; and
(v) past services under section 9 of the Administration of Justice Act 1982.

[...]

Solatium [pursuer's arguments]

[29] In relation to solatium for pain and suffering Mr Blessing submitted that there should be an award of £25,000 with interest

on two-thirds of that sum (two-thirds being attributed to the past).

[30] In support of his submission, Mr Blessing referred me to the Judicial Studies Board Guideline for the Assessment of General Damages in Personal Injuries Cases, Chapter 6, section B ("Back Injuries"). It was suggested that paragraphs (a) ("severe") (iii) was appropriate. Paragraph (a)(ii) was too high. Paragraph (b) ("moderate") (ii) was too low. Paragraph (b)(i) could be a possibility but no mention is made of how the pursuer changed as a result of the accident.

[31] In the present case, the pursuer suffered a fracture of a vertebral body and he continues to have a level of pain that was described as "surprisingly high". There was no inference that he was not suffering the pain, just that it was surprisingly high. His sex life has been affected and he remains in severe pain and discomfort.

[32] Mr Blessing also provided me with the following references:
- *Leebody* v *Liddle* 2000 SCLR 495 (soft tissue damage due to whiplash: £15,000 adjusted for inflation to £17,400);
- *Kumar* v *Kumar*, 1997 Kemp and Kemp F5-014 (crush fracture and serious soft tissue injury to spinal ligament; £18,000 adjusted for inflation to £22,500);
- *Scully* v *Hoogstraten*, 1993, from Butterworths Quantum No 948 (crush fracture; £10,000 adjusted for inflation to £14,000);
- *Mulroy* v *Garland*, from Butterworths Quantum No 970 (anterior wedge fracture of T12 and L1 £20,000 adjusted for inflation to £25,800).

[...]

Solatium [defenders' arguments]

[74] Ms Hodge submitted that an award of £10,000 would be appropriate for solatium (two-thirds being attributed to the past).

[75] The defenders placed solatium in the range described in the Judicial Studies Board Guidelines for the Assessment of General Damages in Personal Injuries Cases, Chapter 6, section B ("Back Injuries"), paragraph (b) ("moderate") (ii).

[76] I was also referred to:
- *Dall* v *Gaughan* 2004 SCLR 1073 (£11,000 adjusted for inflation to £11,500); and

- *Emslie* v *Bell* 12 August 2004, Lord Menzies (£12,000 adjusted for inflation to £12,300).

[77] Ms Hodge indicated that she had at first been drawn to paragraph (b)(i) of the Judicial Studies Board Guidelines but, having further considered the circumstances and the consequences for the pursuer, she considered that paragraph (b)(ii) was more appropriate.

[...]

Solatium [Judge's decision]

[109] On the evidence, at the end of the day, there was little real difference between the medical experts although there were some differences in emphasis.

[110] The pursuer's position was fairly summarised by Mr Blessing (as outlined above). In my view, the differences in emphasis are best resolved by accepting Mr McMaster's evidence – as Mr Blessing suggested.

[111] Mr McMaster's opinion and prognosis (in his report No 6/8 of Process) was to the following effect:

> "(The pursuer) is now in a stable stage and there will be no further improvement. He will always have some degree of mild intermittent discomfort in his back aggravated by stressful activities and will not be fit to return to his previous heavy manual work. However he appears well motivated with regard to work and should be capable of moderate activities which do not require repeated heavy lifting from a low level and he will find it difficult to work in awkward or confined spaces. He should be able to walk as far as is necessary but it will be uncomfortable to be in one position sitting or standing for more than 30 to 40 minutes without being given the opportunity to move around for a short period. Theoretically, it is possible that he could develop increasing degenerative arthritic changes in his back at the site of the fracture over a prolonged number of years but this is unlikely to cause any significant deterioration in his present level of pain or disability."

[112] In my opinion, in the whole circumstances and having regard to the competing submissions of the parties, the appropriate award for solatium for pain and suffering in this case is £18,000.

[113] Interest will run on two-thirds of that sum (attributed to the past) at 4 per cent.

[...]

[Spreadsheet showing final computation of all damages]

APPENDIX 3
HOW MUCH FOR A LEG?

The following shows different awards under different systems for various leg injuries. Because the Rogers, *Comparative Perspective* study considered a simple fracture of the tibia from which a full recovery was made within the usual period, such injuries are considered in the other systems. For Scotland there is a femur (and more) case illustrating a part of the exercise for those unfamiliar with the time and effort which goes into such a task. The awards (unless stated) do not include loss of earnings.

Irish Personal Injuries Assessment Board

Upper leg (femur bone)

Fractures

Serious injuries include those where a risk of future arthritis exists and the level of that risk, the recovery period, treatment type and duration and what complications exist, for example fracture non-union or limb shortening. Fractures that involve a joint are usually considered more complicated than others due to the increased impact on limb movement.

(Illustrative currency conversions as at 6/2/2008).

Substantially recovered: €19,600 [£14,617] to €35,000 [£26,103]
Significant ongoing: €26,700 [£19,913]to €60,000 [£44,748]
Serious and permanent conditions: €49,200 [£36,693] to €79,800 [£59,515]

Lower leg (tibia and fibula bones)

Fractures

This category includes fractures to both the tibia and fibula. A fracture to the fibula is usually not as severe as that of a tibia. Fractures that involve a joint are usually considered more complicated than others due to the increased impact on limb movement. Complications may arise such as fractures of both bones, which may include vein damage, soft tissue damage, malunion, delayed union and non-union and joint stiffness at either the ankle or knee or both. Open fractures (where the bone(s) break the skin) may be further complicated by infection. Peripheral nerve damage (peroneal nerve) may also be associated with the fractures.

(Illustrative currency conversion as at 15/2/08)

Substantially recovered: €15,400 [£11,526] to €34,600 [£25,894]

Significant ongoing: €21,300 [£15,940] to €73,900 [£55,314]
Serious and permanent conditions: €47,500 [£35,556] to €87,300 [£65,358]

UK Criminal Injuries Compensation Authority

(the number in brackets is the level number)

Femur (thigh bone)

Fractured
    one leg
        substantial recovery (8) £3,800
        continuing significant disability (11) £6,600
    both legs
        substantial recovery (10) £5,500
        continuing significant disability (13) £11,000

Fibula (slender bone from knee to ankle)

Fractured
    one leg
        substantial recovery (6) £2,500
        continuing significant disability (8) £3,800
    both legs
        substantial recovery (7) £3,300
        continuing significant disability (10) £5,500

Tibia (shin bone)

Fractured
    one leg
        substantial recovery (8) £3,800
        continuing significant disability (11) £6,600
    both legs
        substantial recovery (10) £5,500
        continuing significant disability (13) £11,000

English Judicial Studies Board Guidelines (8th edn)

[Although being only guidance, something very like the process illustrated below for Scotland will be followed, subject to the cost constraints of the Woolf reforms].
(L)
…

(b) Severe Leg Injuries

(i) The most serious injuries short of amputation: £56,000 to £79,000

Some injuries, although not involving amputation, are so severe that the courts have awarded damages at a comparable level. Such injuries would include extensive degloving of the leg, where there is gross shortening of the leg or where fractures have not united and extensive bone grafting has been undertaken.

(ii) Very Serious: £32,000 to £49,350.

Injuries leading to permanent problems with mobility, the need for crutches for the remainder of the injured person's life; injuries where multiple fractures have taken years to heal and have led to serious deformity and limitation of movement, or where arthritis has developed in a joint so that further surgical treatment is likely.

(iii) Serious: £22,650 to £32,000

Serious injuries to joints or ligaments resulting in instability, prolonged treatment, a lengthy period of non-weight-bearing, the near certainty that arthritis will ensue; injuries involving the hip, requiring arthrodesis or hip replacement, extensive scarring. To justify an award within this bracket a combination of such features will generally be necessary.

(iv) Moderate: £16,300 to £22,650

This bracket includes severe, complicated or multiple fractures. The level of an award within the bracket will be influenced by the period off work; the presence or risk of degenerative changes; imperfect union of fractures, muscle wasting, limited joint movement; instability in the knee; unsightly scarring or permanently increased vulnerability to future damage.

(8) Less Serious Leg injuries

(i) Fractures from which an incomplete recovery is made: £10,500 to £16,300.

The injured person will be left with a metal implant and/or defective gait, a limp, impaired mobility, sensory loss, discomfort or an exacerbation of a pre-existing disability.

(ii) Simple fracture of a femur with no damage to articular surfaces £5,350 to £8,150

[Note – no narrative in original]

(iii) Simple fractures and soft tissue injuries: up to £5,350.

At the top of the bracket will come simple fractures of the tibia or fibula from which a complete recovery has been made. Below this level fall a wide variety of soft-tissue injuries, lacerations, cuts, bruising or contusions, all of which have recovered completely or almost so and any residual disability is cosmetic or of a minor nature.

Europe

The Rogers, *Comparative Perspective* study asked in its initial questionnaire for approximate figures or a range of figures for particular injuries sustained by a 30-year-old plaintiff (XVII). Question (e) related to a simple fracture of the tibia with full recovery within the normal period. (The matter of a period is important for those systems which utilise day rates for calculating the award.)

Austria
ATS 650,000 (based on a previous case).

Belgium
€9,375. This was based on a previous case but on the basis of 25 per cent permanent invalidity which is not what would be considered a full recovery here. The award for the time in hospital and pain is recorded as €19.

England
€7,500 (based on JSB).

France
FF 15,000.

Germany
€2,000–€2,500.

Greece
So impressionistic that it was impossible to give any guidance at all.

Italy
No figure because it would be calculated as a temporary impairment percentage multiplied by the number of days.

Netherlands
€500–€1,100.

Spain
Difficult to find a "simple" figure from the courts but there is one for the tibia of a baby – €2,404; and the statutory RTA tariff includes pecuniary loss so including that and taking a 45-day period of temporary incapacity the award would be – €1,758.

No direct comparison can be made with these figures – they are out of date and would need adjusted for local inflation and converted at current rates. Rogers demonstrates in "Comparative Report" in Rogers, *Comparative Perspective* (at p 271) that it is necessary too to consider the buying power of an award and does this convincingly with a table based on using Zurich as a baseline of 100. The effect of tax on awards may have an effect too. The PIAB was not in existence at the time of Rogers, *Comparative Perspective*, but as can be seen above the figure there would be: Substantially recovered €15,400 [£11,526] to €34,600 [£25,894].

THE PROCESS OF ASSESSING AN INJURY IN SCOTS LAW

Stage 1: Find a list of relevant cases from either *McEwan & Paton* or *Bennett*.

Stage 2: Find a case like the following, read it and make notes; thereafter proceed to Stage 3.

Lamont v *Cameron's Executrix* 1997 SLT 1147
(Lord Rodger, Outer House)

Mrs Judith Lamont raised an action against Mrs Sheila Cameron, the executrix and widow of the late Ian Cameron, for damages for injuries sustained in a road accident. The accident happened on 29 January 1992 when the pursuer was aged 25. Liability was admitted and the case came to proof on quantum before the Lord Ordinary (Rodger). In awarding damages of £68,050 plus interest, his Lordship said:

> "The pursuer was born in 1967 and was 29 years of age at the date of the proof …

History of the pursuer's condition

The pursuer was seriously injured in the accident. Indeed Mr Brian Dean, the consultant orthopaedic surgeon who treated her, described her injuries as life threatening and this was not disputed by the defender's counsel. Some initial treatment was given at the scene but the pursuer was then taken to the accident and emergency department at the Victoria hospital, Kirkcaldy. According to Mr Dean, the pursuer was found to be in a state of shock and there was difficulty in maintaining an airway because of her injuries. Mr Barry O'Regan, the consultant oral and maxillo facial surgeon who treated the pursuer, provided reports which were treated as being equivalent to evidence by him. In his report dated 14 April 1992 Mr O'Regan described her condition on admission in these terms:

> 'The patient had extensive soft tissue injuries on the right side of the face. In particular she had a jagged laceration which extended down to bone over the right fronto-zygomatic region. This was "L" shaped and 21¼ cms in length. There were further diffuse abrasions and minor puncture wounds over the skin of the right cheek and adjacent lateral aspect of the orbit which contained grit and other debris from the accident site.
>
> The patient's skeletal injuries consisted of a grossly displaced and comminuted fracture of the right orbital complex with obvious involvement of the lateral orbital wall, inferior orbital rim, and orbital floor. Correspondingly the pupil level on the right side was lowered and there was evidence of gross diplopia and restriction of ocular movement.
>
> Radiographic examination confirmed the clinical impression of gross comminution and displacement of the orbital complex, particularly on the lateral and inferior aspect of the orbit.'

The pursuer also had a fracture of the shaft of the left femur.

On the day of her admission the pursuer underwent a first operation under general anaesthetic. Mr O'Regan records that primary debridement of the pursuer's facial wounds was carried out and closure of the laceration over the right FZ suture was achieved. Further lacerations over the right cheek and upper lip were closed simultaneously and inter-oral lacerations identified under anaesthesia were also sutured. The shaft of the femur was treated by closed intramedullary nailing and locking screws.

At 8.15 pm the pursuer was admitted to the intensive care unit. The pursuer's condition was extremely painful: she suffered pain in both her face and her leg. When in the accident and emergency department she was given diamorphine to ease her pain and the notes record that, in the period which followed, the pursuer was sick on a number of occasions – this was due to the pain – and was given diamorphine. Indeed she continued to receive infusions of diamorphine until 1 February.

It had not been possible at the time of the first operation to deal definitively with the injury to the pursuer's eye, but over the next few days clinical examination revealed that the pursuer had right infra-orbital nerve anaesthesia and there was displacement and comminution of the right orbital rim with gross diplopia, especially on upward and downward gaze. It was noted that the pursuer's right pupil was depressed to the extent of 2 to 3 mm and there was limitation of eye movement. X-ray examination confirmed a comminuted orbital complex injury with clear evidence of orbital rim and floor comminution. The pursuer therefore had to undergo a further operation on 7 February when her orbit was reconstructed. Stainless steel wires were applied to the segments at the orbital rim and a sialastic graft was placed in the orbital floor *1148 following retrieval of the soft tissues which had prolapsed into the maxillary sinus.

Happily the pursuer made a good recovery and she was able to be discharged on 13 February when her mother and father helped to look after her. The pursuer required to use crutches. She attended out-patient clinics of both the Victoria and Dunfermline and West Fife hospitals. Although by the time she left hospital the pursuer's pain had resolved substantially, unfortunately she continued to suffer pain at the fracture site in her leg. The pursuer described how she had constant pain from her broken leg and incidents of acute pain. An operation was carried out under general anaesthetic on 6 March 1992 when a further cross screw was inserted into her femur to stabilise the fracture. On this occasion she was in hospital for two days. Thereafter the fracture of the shaft of the femur healed. Unfortunately by 5 October 1992 the pursuer was complaining of pain and discomfort in the proximal end of the nail. She could not lie on her left side in bed. This discomfort continued and on 5 March 1993 an operation was carried out, again under general anaesthesia, in which the old incision was excised and the cross screw was removed. The pursuer remained in hospital overnight. Thereafter the pain in her hip was much reduced, though the pursuer continues to suffer a permanent ache in her thigh, particularly if pressure is exerted at the site of the fracture. She does not limp. The pursuer described how, in about 1994, she would suffer episodes of acute pain which would come on suddenly when something clicked. She might have to hold on to someone else until the episode passed. Moreover, when she was about to kneel and was bending her knees acutely, she would experience a shooting pain in her left knee. These complaints are reflected on the first page of Mr Dean's report of his examination of the pursuer on 13 June 1994. According to the pursuer she still gets a shooting pain in her hip now and again and she finds this worrying. She continues to have discomfort when kneeling and tenderness on her thigh. Occasionally she has a sore leg at the end of the day. I refer also to the history recorded by Mr McRae in section 4 of his report.

Mr Dean summarised his opinion of the pursuer's condition when he saw her in June 1994 by saying that she undoubtedly had restriction of movement of:

> '1 Left hip joint. This is in part due to scarring of soft tissues around the greater trochanter following insertion of intramedullary nail and a degree of heterotopic calcification in this region. Movements however are painful. Undoubtedly significant forces were transmitted through

the hip at the time of original injury. It is my opinion that in view of this lady's continuing symptoms related to her hip joint, on the grounds of probability, it is estimated that there is a 30–40 per cent chance of her developing arthritis as a result of injury.

2 Injury to knee. Again this lady has significant tenderness in and around the patella and in the retropatellar region with some curtailment of full flexion of the knee causing difficulties with kneeling. Again, significant forces were transmitted through the flexed knee when the initial accident took place and, again, it is estimated, on the grounds of probability, that there is a 30–40 per cent chance of this lady developing arthritis in her knee.'

I must return shortly to the question of possible arthritis. Mr Dean envisaged that in the future the pursuer would have to undergo a further operation for the removal of the nail. Mr McRae was of the same opinion. I therefore proceed on the basis that the pursuer will indeed have to undergo a further operation under general anaesthesia to round off her orthopaedic treatment.

The pursuer has cosmetically obvious scarring over the lateral aspect of the left hip region. That scar is subject to keloid formation. This scarring will be permanent. There are also two small scars at the lateral aspect of the lower end of the pursuer's thigh, where the cross screws were inserted. These scars are well healed and are not cosmetically obvious. There is a further area of scarring in the pretibial region of the pursuer's left leg, but that is only minimally cosmetically obvious. On her right leg there is a J-shaped scar on the upper third of the anterolateral aspect of the lower leg, measuring 1½ inches in length. The scar is well healed, but it is cosmetically obvious and must be considered permanent.

Very fortunately the operation on her eye proved a great success and not only has the pursuer no residual double vision but she also has a full range of eye movements. The only symptom which she now has in this connection is a certain alteration in sensation in her upper lip and the adjacent mucosa – this can be experienced when the pursuer drinks hot fluids and also when her husband kisses her. Mr O'Regan describes the pursuer as suffering from 'minor residual aesthetic deformity' due to a slight roughening of the skin and of the right upper and lower lid of her right eye, and in evidence the pursuer accepted that description, though she indicated that she planned to have a further cosmetic operation to try to improve these matters.

In cross examination the pursuer assented to a summary of her history along the following lines. In the accident she suffered face and leg injuries. She spent over two weeks in hospital and then spent time with her parents. After seven months she was fit to return to work. The complaints which she now has do not ruin her life: they are unpleasant and niggles, more than anything else. I should add, however, that it is clear that, even after the pursuer returned to work, she continued to suffer pain. She also has a certain amount of scarring which I have described already.

This brief survey of the history of the pursuer's condition should vouch two points, which were not really in dispute between the parties. First, the pursuer suffered very serious injuries which were extremely painful to begin with and which were not only potentially life threatening, but also affected her eyesight. Secondly, the pursuer has made a remarkably good recovery. This is not something which redounds to the credit of the defender, of course, but rather is due to the care and skill of the medical practitioners who have treated the pursuer. In addition the pursuer came over in evidence as someone who has a forceful personality and who would have done everything to advance her own recovery. Putting the matter negatively and at its very least, as the defender's expert, Mr McRae, noted, the pursuer 'showed no tendency to exaggeration or embellishment'. All this means that the claim for damages is a claim by someone who has made an excellent recovery and therefore is left with far fewer problems than might have been expected. The complications in assessing the pursuer's claim relate in particular to her employment and to this I must now turn.

[...]

I had no hesitation in accepting the thrust of the pursuer's evidence on these matters. She is clearly an intelligent and go ahead lady who, like many other women of her generation, would have intended to carry on the career for which she had trained – as she put it in a slightly different context, she had been a long time at university just to throw it away. While she would have taken time off to have her family, she would have made the necessary childminding arrangements to make sure that she could carry on with her job. While it is, of course, impossible to say precisely what position she would have attained by this stage, I accept that she would have had more experience from full time practice and so would have been further on with her career and in a better position to apply for other jobs. This effect on her career will not simply have reduced the earnings which she has actually made but will also have had some impact on her present ability to obtain a good position with prospects for the future. Any difficulty caused might be compounded, as I have already indicated, by her reluctance to drive long distances or unfamiliar routes.

General impact of the accident

Before the accident the pursuer had lived an active life: she had been a member of a sports club and had enjoyed riding, badminton and swimming. Since the accident she has swum a bit to build up the muscles in her leg, but she is self conscious about the scar on the side of her leg. She has played a little badminton but has not gone back to riding since she thinks that she would find the process of mounting a horse painful. In general she considers that she is not so fit as she was before the accident. She also used to go dancing but does not do so now: she very readily conceded that this might be due to the fact that her social life is circumscribed by the need to look after the baby rather than to any effect of the accident. On a somewhat broader front the pursuer considers that before the accident she was a confident young professional, rushing about and outgoing, whereas now she is not as outgoing or confident. In part at least she associates this with a concern about her appearance: for instance she now watches the light she is standing in. The pursuer's sister, Mrs Forsyth, said that she had noticed a change in the pursuer since the accident. Previously she had been very open and assertive, very outgoing. According to her sister, the pursuer is now less confident in social situations, now tends to take more of a back seat and adopts a more fatalistic attitude.

On the other hand, watching the pursuer in the witness box, I have to say that I could not really detect any lack of confidence. Certainly, by comparison with many people who give evidence, she was particularly calm, clear and firm. At times she made replies which showed that she was fully aware of a humorous aspect of some observation which she had made or which counsel had made. All in all I considered that she came over as a lively and attractive person. In that connection I was interested to notice that the defender's orthopaedic surgeon, Mr McRae, writing of his impression when he examined the pursuer on 6 September 1995, observed that 'her personality came across as being vivacious and outgoing, and she showed no evidence of anxiety, distress or depression'. In view of the evidence of the pursuer and her sister, I am prepared to accept that the pursuer may not be quite so outgoing or confident as she once was. It may be that the pursuer feels that in some way she has been diminished. Whether she is in fact in any way diminished I find it impossible to say. On the other hand the pursuer's personality at present struck me as eminently attractive and she did not appear in any way unable to handle the very difficult role of giving evidence and talking about her experiences and even her feelings. Therefore even if the pursuer's personality has been changed to a certain extent, it certainly has not been changed in any way which disables her for ordinary society or for the world of professional work. Indeed it was noteworthy that at no point did the pursuer or her sister suggest that the pursuer had any psychological difficulty in carrying on her veterinary work which must require her to take numberless decisions and involve constant contact with members of the public looking for advice.

I turn now to consider the various heads of damages claimed.

Solatium

The pursuer has a claim for solatium for pain and suffering both in the past and in the future. So far as the future is concerned, the pursuer seeks an award of solatium on the basis that there is a risk that at some time she will develop arthritis. The defender says that this risk can now be discounted. This question must be addressed before the pursuer's claim for solatium can be assessed. The dispute really hinges on a difference of opinion between the pursuer's expert, Mr Dean, and the defender's expert, Mr McRae."

His Lordship then gave his reasons for preferring the opinion of Mr McRae and continued:

"Accepting his evidence, I have reached the view that there is no significant risk of the pursuer developing arthritis in either the hip or the knee. It is on this basis, accordingly, that I now turn to assess the damages for solatium.

While acknowledging that they could provide only limited help, counsel referred me to a number of cases in the hope that they would provide guidance on the quantification of the pursuer's claim for solatium. Counsel for the pursuer cited *Prentice* v *William Thyne Ltd* 1989 SLT 336; *MacAngus* v *Harry Lawson Ltd* 1981 SLT (Notes) 94; *Barker* v *Murdoch*, 1977 SLT (Notes) 75; and *Power* v *Kitchener*, Kemp and Kemp, para C2–037. Counsel for the pursuer submitted that, having regard to all the circumstances, including the considerable initial pain, the number of operations which have been performed and the two operations which are likely still to lie ahead, as well as to the effect of the injury on the pursuer's self confidence and her ability to drive, an appropriate award would be £25,000 of which three quarters would relate to the past. Counsel for the defender referred me to *Clarke* v *McFadyen* 1990 SLT 277; *Morrison* v *Barton* 1994 SLT 653 and 657; and *Blackhall* v *MacInnes* 1997 SLT 649. She also drew my attention to the publication of the Judicial Studies Board, Guidelines for the Assessment of General Damages in Personal Injuries Cases (2nd edn 1994), especially p 36 (iii)–(v). For her part counsel for the defender argued that, if I accepted Mr McRae's evidence, then the award of damages should fall into the range between £7,500 and £ 11,500.

In the light of the authorities and in view of my decision on the arthritis point, I consider that the level of award suggested by counsel for the pursuer is too high, having regard to the excellent recovery which the pursuer has made. Nonetheless I take account of the continuing psychological impact of the accident on the pursuer and I bear in mind that she is likely to undergo two further operations. I consider that an award of £10,000 for solatium would be appropriate of which I would allocate 90 per cent to the past.

Patrimonial loss

[…]

I award £10,000 for solatium."

Stage 3:

IF no more analogous cases

THEN synthesise notes based on these previous cases and form a view and prepare a note of argument;

OTHERWISE go back to Stage 2.

APPENDIX 4

A RECONSTRUCTION OF THE CICA 2001 TARIFF OF SELECTED LISTED INJURIES
(ALLOCATED UP TO £4,400 BY VALUE RATHER THAN BY INJURY)

Level 1 injuries (£1,000)

Multiple Minor injuries. [Minor multiple physical injuries will qualify for compensation only where the applicant has sustained at least three separate physical injuries of the type illustrated below, at least one of which must still have had significant residual effects 6 weeks after the incident. The injuries must also have necessitated at least two visits to or by a medical practitioner within that 6-week period. Examples of qualifying injuries are: (a) grazing, cuts, lacerations (no permanent scarring); (b) severe and widespread bruising; (c) severe soft tissue injury (no permanent disability); (d) black eye(s); (e) bloody nose; (f) hair pulled from scalp; (g) loss of fingernail.]

Ear – fractured mastoid.

Deafness – temporary partial deafness, lasting 6–13 weeks.

Tinnitus (ringing noise in ear(s)), lasting 6–13 weeks.

Blurred or double vision – temporary, lasting 6–13 weeks.

Clicking jaw – temporary, lasting 6–13 weeks.

Neck – fractured hyoid (bone in windpipe).

Strained neck or whiplash injury – disabling for 6–13 weeks.

Nose – deviated nasal septum – no operation.

Fracture of nasal bones – undisplaced.

Fracture/disclocation – one finger other than index finger – one hand – substantial recovery .

Arm – tendon and ligament – minor damage – one arm – substantial recovery.

Sprained – one wrist – disabling for 6–13 weeks.

Strained back – disabling – for 6–13 weeks.

Rib – fractured (or bruised where significant pain lasts more than 6 weeks) – one rib.

Sprained – one ankle – disabling for at least 6–13 weeks.

Patella (knee cap) – dislocated – one knee – substantial recovery.

Leg tendon and ligament – minor damage – one leg – substantial recovery.

Toe – fractured – two or more toes (not great toe) – one foot – substantial recovery.

Loss of one toe (other than great toe).

Level 2 injuries (£1,250)

Teeth – damage to – tooth/teeth requiring root-canal treatment.

Fractured/chipped tooth/teeth requiring treatment.

Loss of tooth/teeth other than front – one tooth.

Slackening of teeth requiring dental treatment.

Upper limbs – scarring – minor disfigurement.

Fracture/disclocation – two or more fingers other than index finger – one hand – substantial recovery.

Torso – scarring – minor disfigurement.

Lower limbs – scarring – minor disfigurement.

Level 3 injuries (£1,500)

Peripheral sensory nerve damage – lasting more than 13 weeks – substantial recovery expected.

Peripheral sensory nerve damage – lasting more than 13 weeks – permanent disability – minor loss.

Burns – neck – minor disfigurement.

Scarring – head – minor visible disfigurement.

Scarring – face – minor disfigurement.

Scarring – neck – minor disfigurement.

Brain – balance impaired – lasting 6–28 weeks.

Concussion – lasting at least 1 week.

Deafness – temporary partial deafness – lasting more than 13 weeks.

Ear – vestibular damage (causing giddiness) – lasting 6–28 weeks.

Hyphaema requiring operation – one eye.

Clicking jaw – temporary – lasting more than 13 weeks.

Face numbness/loss of feeling – temporary lasting more than 13 weeks – recovery expected.

Fracture of nasal bones – displaced.

Teeth – damage to – front tooth/teeth requiring crown(s) .

Loss of crowns.

Upper limbs – burns – minor.

Torso – burns – minor.

Rib – fractured (or bruised where significant pain lasts more than 6 weeks) – two or more.

Lower limbs – burns – minor.

Toe fractured – two or more toes (not great toe) – both feet – substantial recovery.

Level 4 injuries (£1,750)

Perforated ear drum – one ear.

Blurred or double vision – temporary – lasting more than 13 weeks – recovery expected.

Loss of front tooth/teeth (incisor or canine) – one front tooth.

Loss of tooth/teeth other than front – two or more teeth.

Fracture/dislocation – index finger – one hand – substantial recovery.

Fracture/dislocation – one finger other than index finger – both hands – substantial recovery.

Shoulder dislocated – one shoulder – substantial recovery.

Genitalia – injury requiring medical treatment – no significant permanent damage.

Level 5 injuries (£2,000)

Burns – face – minor disfigurement.

Burns – head – minor visible disfigurement.

Epilepsy – post-traumatic epileptic fits – substantial recovery.

Corneal abrasions.

Degeneration of optic nerve – one eye.

Dislocated jaw – substantial recovery.

Fractured ethmoid – no operation.

Fractured zygoma (malar/cheek bone) – no operation – substantial recovery.

Nose – deviated nasal septum – requiring septoplasty.

Fracture of nasal bones – displaced – requiring manipulation or rhinoplasty or turbinectomy.

Tongue – impaired speech – slight.

Fracture/dislocation of thumb – one hand – substantial recovery.

Fracture/dislocation – one finger other than index finger – one hand – continuing significant disability.

Fractured hand – one hand – substantial recovery.

Frozen shoulder (one) – substantial recovery.

Arms – tendon and ligament – minor damage – both arms – substantial recovery.

Arms – tendon and ligament – moderate damage – one arm – substantial recovery.

Sprained – both wrists – disabling for 6–13 weeks.

Clavicle (collar bone) – dislocated acromioclavicular joint.

Fractured clavicle – substantial recovery.

Sprained – both ankles – disabling for at least 6–13 weeks.

Knee arthroscopy (investigative surgery/repair to knee) – no fracture.

Leg tendon and ligament – minor damage – both legs – substantial recovery.

Leg – tendon and ligament moderate damage – one leg – substantial recovery.

Level 6 injuries (£2,500)

Perforated ear drum – both ears.

Glaucoma.

Hyphaema requiring operation – both eyes.

Retina – damage not involving detachment – one eye.

Significant penetrating injury – one eye.

Traumatic angle recession.

Fractured zygoma (malar/cheek bone) – operation required – substantial recovery.

Strained neck or whiplash injury – disabling for more than 13 weeks.

Skull Fracture – simple – no operation.

Fractured tooth/teeth requiring apicectomy – (surgery to gum to reach root – root resection).

Loss of two or three front teeth.

Fracture dislocation – two or more fingers other than index finger – one hand – continuing significant disability.

Partial loss of finger other than thumb or index finger.

Arm – tendon and ligament – minor damage – one arm – continuing significant disability.

Sprained – one wrist – disabling for more than 13 weeks.

Scarring – significant disfigurement.

Back – fracture of vertebra – one vertebra – substantial recovery.

Strained back – disabling – for more than 13 weeks.

Coccyx (tail bone) – fractured.

Scapula (shoulder blade) – fractured – one scapula – substantial recovery.

Sternum (breast bone) – fractured – substantial recovery.

Lower limbs – scarring – significant disfigurement.

Sprained – one ankle – disabling for more than 13 weeks.

Fibula (slender bone from knee to ankle) – fractured – one leg – substantial recovery.

Foot – fractured metatarsal bones – one foot – substantial recovery.

Patella (knee cap) – dislocated – both knees – substantial recovery.

Fractured – one knee – substantial recovery.

Toe fractured – great toe – one foot – substantial recovery.

Toe fractured – two or more toes (not great toe) – one foot – continuing significant disability.

Partial loss of great toe.

Upper limbs – scarring – significant disfigurement.

Level 7 injuries (£3,300)

Peripheral sensory nerve damage – lasting more than 13 weeks – permanent disability – significant loss (eg loss of sensation in large area of leg).

Scarring – head – significant disfigurement.

Scarring – neck – significant disfigurement.

Brain balance – impaired – lasting over 28 weeks – recovery expected.

Tinnitus (ringing noise in ear(s)) – lasting more than 13 weeks.

Ear – Vestibular damage (causing giddiness) – lasting over 28 weeks – recovery expected.

Eye – blow-out or other fracture of orbital bone cavity containing eyeball – no operation.

Cataracts – one eye – requiring operation.

Residual central floater(s) affecting vision.

Fractured mandible and/or maxilla (jaw bones) – no operation – substantial recovery.

Numbness/loss of feeling – permanent – moderate, eg cheek, forehead.

Elbow – dislocated/fractured – one elbow – substantial recovery.

Fracture/dislocation – two or more fingers other than index finger – both hands – substantial recovery.

Humerus (upper arm bone) – fractured – one arm – substantial recovery.

Radius (a forearm bone) – fractured – one arm – substantial recovery.

Frozen – both shoulders – substantial recovery

Arm – tendon and ligament severely damaged – one arm – substantial recovery.

Ulna (a forearm bone) – fractured – one arm – substantial recovery.

Wrist – fractured/dislocated – including scaphoid fracture – one wrist – substantial recovery.

Lung – punctured – one lung.

Fibula (slender bone from knee to ankle) – fractured – both legs – substantial recovery.

Foot – fractured metatarsal bones – both feet – substantial recovery.

Fractured tarsal bones – one foot – substantial recovery.

Fractured heel bone – one foot – substantial recovery.

Leg – tendon and ligament – minor damage – one leg – continuing significant disability.

Leg – tendon and ligament – severe damage – one leg – substantial recovery.

Level 8 injuries (£3,800)

Partial deafness (remaining hearing socially useful, with hearing aid if necessary) – one ear.

Fractured mandible and/or maxilla (jaw bones) – operation required – substantial recovery.

Loss of front tooth/teeth (incisor or canine) – four or more front teeth.

Fracture/dislocation – index finger – one hand – continuing significant disability.

Fracture – both hands – substantial recovery.

Shoulder dislocated – both shoulders – substantial recovery.

Sprained – both wrists – disabling for more than 13 weeks.

Abdomen – injury requiring laparotomy.

Hernia.

Lung collapsed – one lung.

Sprained – both ankles – disabling for more than 13 weeks.

Level 9 injuries (£4,400)

Burns – head – moderate.

Scarring – face – significant disfigurement.

Brain haemorrhage/stroke – substantial recovery.

Subdural or extradural haematoma – treated conservatively.

Loss of ear – partial loss of ear(s).

Eye – blow-out or other fracture of orbital bone cavity containing eyeball – requiring operation.

Blurred or double vision – permanent – slight.

Fractured zygoma (malar/cheek bone) – no operation – continuing significant disability.

Face numbness/loss of feeling – severe, eg lip interfering with function.

Partial loss of nose (at least 10 per cent) .

Skull fracture – depressed – no operation.

Upper limbs – burns – moderate.

Fracture/dislocation of thumb – one hand – continuing significant disability.

Fracture/dislocation – index finger – both hands – substantial recovery.

Fracture/dislocation – one finger other than index finger – both hands – continuing significant disability.

Partial loss of thumb or index finger.

Arms – tendon and ligament – minor damage – both arms – continuing significant disability.

Arm – tendon and ligament – moderate damage – one arm – continuing significant disability.

Arm – tendon and ligament – moderate damage – both arms – substantial recovery.

Burns – moderate.

Back – fracture of vertebra – more than one vertebra – substantial recovery.

Fractured – two clavicles – substantial recovery.

Pelvis – fractured – substantial recovery.
Scapula (shoulder blade) – fractured – one scapula – continuing significant disability.
Scapula (shoulder blade) – fractured – two scapulas – substantial recovery.
Loss of spleen.
Lower limbs – burns – moderate.
Ankle – fractured or dislocated – one ankle – substantial recovery.
Hip – fractured/dislocated – one hip – substantial recovery.
Fractured – both knees – substantial recovery.
Legs – tendon and ligament – both legs – substantial recovery.
Toe – fractured – two or more toes (not great toe) – both feet – continuing significant disability.
Loss of two or more toes (other than great toes).

APPENDIX 5
WHAT PEOPLE SAY THE DAMAGES SHOULD BE

[Damages for Personal Injury: Non-pecuniary Loss, Law Com No 257. (1999). Extract from Regional Table, answers to Case D, from Appendix B: Research Carried Out by the Office for National Statistics Into Public Perceptions of What Damages for Non-pecuniary Loss in Personal Injury Cases Should Be ("ONS"). [Note: data obtained September/November 1998]

CASE D

A 34-year-old woman suffered an injury to her neck in a road traffic accident. She could not drive or work for 2 weeks because of pain and stiffness in her neck. She had regular severe headaches for about 3 weeks, after which they occurred less often. Her symptoms had disappeared 18 months after her accident, but she has given up keep-fit and is a less confident driver.

Question: How much money do you think the 34-year-old woman in Case D should receive to compensate her for things other than her financial loss?

Level of damages	Total	Scotland
Up to and including £100	10%	11%
£101 to £1,000	12%	12%
£1,001 to £3,500	16%	11%
£3,501 to £4,999	1%	1%
£5,000 to £6,999	15%	17%
£7,000 to £10,000	15%	17%
£10,001 to £20,000	9%	7%
£20,001 to £40,000	5%	8%
Over £40,000	10%	7%
Don't know	7%	9%
Base	*3343*	*262*

BIBLIOGRAPHY

BOOKS; AND CHAPTERS IN BOOKS

Atiyah, P S, *The Damages Lottery* (Hart, 1997).

Bennett, S A, *Personal Injury Damages in Scotland* (Barnstoneworth, 2007) (looseleaf).
Bona, M, and P Mead (eds), *Personal Injury Compensation in Europe* (Kluwer, 2003).

Calabresi, G, *The Costs of Accidents: A Legal and economic analysis* (Yale University Press, 1970).
Cane, P, *Atiyah's Accidents, Compensation and the Law* (7th edn, Cambridge University Press, 2006).
Conway, R, *Personal Injury Practice in the Sheriff Court* (2nd edn, W Green, 2003).
Cooper, T (Lord) (ed; trans) *Regiam Majestatem* (Stair Society), vol 11.

Hajducki, A, *Civil Jury Trials* (2nd edn, Avizandum, 2006).

Lee, E, *et al*, *Compensation Crazy: Do we blame and claim too much?* (Institute of Ideas, Hodder & Stoughton, 2002).

McIntosh, D, and M Holmes (eds), *Personal Injury Awards in EU and EFTA Countries* (3rd edn, Kluwer, 2003).
McKenzie, D, and R Evans-Jones, "The Development of Remedies for Personal Injuries and Death" in R Evans Jones (ed), *The Civil Law Tradition in Scotland* (Stair Society, Supplementary volume 2, 1995), p 284.
Markesinis, B, *et al*, *Compensation for Personal Injury in English, German and Italian Law: A Comparative Outline* (Cambridge University Press, 2005).
Marsh, R, and F Zuleeg, "The Scottish Public Sector: Does Size Matter?" (September 2006) Hume Occasional Paper No 69.

Paton, A (The Hon Lady) (ed), *McEwan and Paton on Damages for Personal Injuries in Scotland* (W Green, 1989 to date) (looseleaf).

Rodgers, W V H (ed), *Damages for Non-Pecuniary Loss in a Comparative Perspective* (SpringerWein, 2001).

Walker, D M, *A Legal History of Scotland*, vol II (Tottel, 2001).
———, vol III (Tottel, 2001).
———, vol IV (Tottel, 2001).
Welch, T (ed), *Macphail's Sheriff Court Practice* (3rd edn, 2006).
White, R M, and M J Fletcher, *Delictual Damages* (Butterworths, 2000).

Zimmermann, R, *The Law of Obligations: Roman Foundations of the Civilian Tradition* (Clarendon, 1996) (first published Juta & Co, 1990).

ARTICLES

Beer, J, "Compensation for personal Injury and Human rights: The European Court of Human Rights Monitors the Quality of Compensation Law in the Contracting States", PEOPIL Bulletin, July 2006, 3.

Conway, R, "A Colossus in the room" 2008 (53) JLSS 14.

Duff, P, "The 1996 Criminal Injuries Compensation Scheme" 1996 SLT (News) 221.

Garrett, G, "New Deal for PI Claims" (2005) (Dec) JLSS 28.
———, "A Breach of Protocol" 2008 (Feb) JLSS 14.
Greenleaf, G, "A Colossus come to judgment: GIO's expert system on general damages" (1993) 67 ALJ 220.

Lewis, R, "Insurance and the tort system" (2005) 25 LS 85.

Pollock, A S, "Criminal Injuries Compensation: the Tariff" (1996) 40 JLS 93.

Walker, I, "Criminal Injuries Compensation: A government betrayal" [1994] JPIL 47.

Watson, A, "Personal Injuries in the XII Tables" (1975) 43 *Tijdschrift voor Rechtsgeschiedenis* 213.

Williams, K, "Britain's 'Compensation Culture' Reviewed" (2005) 25 LS 499.

GOVERNMENT, NGO, ORGANISATIONS' REPORTS (DATE ORDER)

Royal Commission on Civil Liability and Compensation for Personal Injury (Pearson Commission) (Cmnd 7054, 1978), 3 vols.

Law Commission, *Damages for Personal Injury: Non-pecuniary Loss* (Law Com No 257, 1999).

Panel of Eminent Persons, *Review of the Law of Negligence Final Report*, October 2002 (Ipp Report).

European Group of Tort Law, *Principles of European Tort Law: Text and Commentary* (SpringerWien, 2005).

Rebuilding Lives – Supporting Victims of Crime (Cm 6705, 2005).

Department for Constitutional Affairs, *Case track limits and the claims process for personal injury claims*, Consultation Paper CP 8/07 20/04/2007.

Scottish Law Commission, *Damages for Wrongful Death* (SLC DP No 135, 2007).

Samuels, E, *Managing Procedure: Evaluation of New Rules for actions of damages for, or arising from, personal injuries in the Court of Session (Chapter 43)* Research Findings, Scottish Parliament, Social Research, Civil Justice, Research Findings 1/2007.

Interim Outline Edition – Draft Common Frame of Reference (DCFR), Principles, Definitions and Model Rules of European Private Law, Von Bar, Clive *et al* (eds) (Sellier, 2008).

Scottish Law Commission, *Report on Damages for Wrongful Death*, (SLC No. 213, 2008).

Report of the Scottish Civil Courts Review, *Scottish Civil Courts Review*, Chair Lord Gill (September 2009).

WEBSITES

Busnelli, F D, "Summary report of work effected by the Jurists Group, Trier, 8–9 June 2000", Institute for European Traffic Law website: http://www.eu-traffic-law.org/ (See "documents" and then "initiatives") (accessed 8/10/09).

PEOPIL's Response to the Recommendations to the Commission on a European Disability Scale, January 2004 http://www.peopil.com/peopil/userfiles/file/BaremeMedicalTablesHarmonisationofdamages Jan2004.pdf (accessed 8/10/09).

PIAB medical reports: http://www.injuriesboard.ie/eng/Forms_and_Publications/ (accessed 8/10/09).

Roberts, E, "Claims before the Personal Injuries Assessment Board Newsletter" A & L Goodbody (December 2005): http://www.algoodbody.ie/ezinelitigation/article.asp?9+56 (accessed 8/10/09).

Rothley Group on the European Scale, Proposed European disability rating scale, produced under the auspices of Confédération Européenne d'Experts en Evaluation et en Réparation du Dommage Corporel (CEREDOC): http://www.ceredoc.eu/. An English translation was available from the Institute for European Traffic Law website: http://www.eu-traffic-law.org/ ("Documents-European Barème") (accessed 8/10/08 but has recently not been accessible).

Hogan, B, *A Cost –Benefit Analysis of the PIAB 2006* (PIAB, 2006): http://www.injuriesboard.ie/eng/Forms_and_Publications/Corporate_Publications/A_Cost_Benifit_Analysis_of_the_Personal_Injuries_Assessment_Board.pdf (accessed 8/10/09).

INDEX

actio iniuriarum, 7
assessment of damages
  alternative methods, 19–28
  analysis of, 29–48
  Criminal Injuries Compensation
    Scheme, 19–21
  examples, finding, 11–13
  fatal claims, in *see* **fatal claims**
  judicial, 13–17
  meaning of, 7–8
  rationale for, 29–31
  state control of, 27–28
  time of, 8–9
assessment of injury
  medical evidence, 36–38, 49
  typical case, 77–83
assessors
  counsel as, 10
  judges as, 9
  jurors as, 10
  legal advisers as, 9
  parties as, 10
  unqualified claims handlers as, 9
Australia
  bespoke assessment method, 24
Austria
  leg injuries, awards for, 76
authorities on quantum, presentation of,
  14–15

***barème* assessment system**
  see also under individual jurisdictions
  bespoke systems with elements of,
    26–27
  European harmonisation and, 43–44
  meaning of, 24
Belgium
  bespoke assessment system, plus
    guidance, 25
  leg injuries, awards for, 76
  terminology in, 7

bespoke assessment system
  barème, plus, 26–27
  generally, 24–25
  official guidance, plus, 25–26
Book of Quantum
  generally, 23
  valuation of claim, 22

CICA *see* **Criminal Injuries
    Compensation Authority**
CICB *see* **Criminal Injuries
    Compensation Board**
claims handlers
  assessors of damages, as, 9
  knowledge levels among, 9–10
**Colossus computerised system, impact
  of,** 34–36
comparative personal injury law,
  4–5
compensation claims
  cost of, 40–41
  regulation of, 40
"compensation culture", 2
**compensation for non-pecuniary aspects
  of injury,** 29–30
contract debt, 6
cost of claims, 40–43
**court-disputed non-pecuniary damages
  (medium value) (JSB use) (other
  disputed issues) (typical case),**
  69–72
**court-disputed non-pecuniary loss
  (low value) (typical case),**
  63–69
criminal injuries compensation
  see also **Criminal Injuries Compensation
    Authority;
    Criminal Injuries Compensation
    Scheme**
  definition, 5

97

Criminal Injuries Compensation
    Authority (CICA)
  see also Criminal Injuries Compensation
    Scheme
  cost of claims, 41
  generally, 19–21
  leg injuries, awards for, 74
  medical reports, acceptance of, 37
  tariff
    Level 1 injuries, 84–85
    Level 2 injuries, 85
    Level 3 injuries, 85–86
    Level 4 injuries, 86
    Level 5 injuries, 86–87
    Level 6 injuries, 87–88
    Level 7 injuries, 88–89
    Level 8 injuries, 89–90
    Level 9 injuries, 90–91
    reconstructing, 47–48
Criminal Injuries Compensation Board
    (CICB), 20
Criminal Injuries Compensation Scheme
  assessment method, 19–21
  pain and suffering, bands for, 20
  tariff, as, 38

damages
  categorisation of, 6–7
  liquidate, 6
  non-pecuniary, 6–7
  schedule of, 14
  unliquidated, 6–7
danno biologico, 7, 27
death
  personal injury, as, 5
  wrongful *see* **wrongful death**
defamation
  delictual nature in Scotland, 7
defender reparation practice, 13
Denmark
  state control of assessment, 27
disability rating scale, proposed European,
    45–46

Eire
  see also Personal Injuries Assessment
    Board
  state control of assessment, 27
England
  see also Judicial Studies Board
  bespoke assessment system, plus
    guidance, 26

England (*cont.*)
  compensation claims
    cost of, 40–41
    regulation of, 40
  leg injuries, awards for, 76
  medical information, 37
European disability rating scale,
    proposed, 45–46
European Group on Tort Law, 43
European harmonisation, 43–47
European jurisdictions
  see also European harmonisation;
    and under individual jurisdictions
  leg injuries, awards for, 76
expert witnesses, 37

fatal claims
  assessment of damages in
    generally, 6
    Scottish Law Commission on, 6
    statutory terminology, 7
  tariff for, proposed, 30–31
"fatal injury"
  definition, 5
Finland
  bespoke assessment system, plus
    guidance, 26
France
  bespoke assessment system plus *barème*,
    26
  leg injuries, awards for, 76
funding of claims, 42–43

Germany
  bespoke assessment system, 25
  leg injuries, awards for, 76
  Schmerzensgeld, 7
Gill Report
  medical information, on, 37
  non-court assessment systems, on,
    56
  Pain and Suffering Damages
    Commission(er), 52–54
  publication of, 4
Gill Review
  background to, 3–4
  cost of litigation, on, 41
  jury trial, retention of, on, 10, 39
  scope of, 4
Greece
  bespoke assessment system, 25
  leg injuries, awards for, 76

INDEX

Greens Weekly Digest
  "Quantum" notes in, 12
  source of assessments, as, 13
human rights
  jury trial and, 11
  tariff imposition and, 32–34
information, sources of
  legal
    jury awards, 10–12
    reported cases, 11–12
    settled actions, 12
    unreported cases, 12
  medical
    haphazard nature of, 36–38, 49
    pre-action protocol on exchange of, 37
information deficit, 34–36
insurance, effect of, 42–43
Internet, the
  source of information on awards, as, 10
Ireland *see* **Eire**
Italy
  bespoke assessment system plus *barème*, 26–27
  danno biologico, 7, 27
  leg injuries, awards for, 76

JSB *see* **Judicial Studies Board**
JSB guidelines
  bespoke assessment system, as, 26
  England, use in, 15
  leg injuries, awards for
    less serious injuries, 75–76
    severe injuries, 75
  Scotland, use in
    categorisation of facts and, 17
    departing from, 52–53
    generally, 15–17, 50–51
    joining, 51–52
    reported cases in, 16–17
    status, 17
    unreported cases, in, 17
judges
  assessors of damages, as, 9
  collegiate nature of, 14–15
  consistency in approaches, 14–15
judicial assessment in Scotland, 13–17
judicial opinions
  sources of assessments, as, 11–12

Judicial Studies Board (JSB)
  guidelines issued by *see* **JSB guidelines**
  judicial training institution, as, 51
Judicial Studies Committee, 51
jurors
  guidance on assessment process, lack of, 10
jury awards
  "rule of thumb" approach, 10–11
  sources of assessments, as, 12
"jury" data, 10–11
jury trial
  assessment at, 10–11
  calibration of awards, 10–11, 39
  Gill Review on, 10
  human rights and, 11
  rationale for, 10–11

leg injuries, awards for
  Austria, in, 76
  Belgium, in, 76
  CICA (UK), 74
  England generally, in, 76
  Europe generally, in, 76
  France, in, 76
  Germany, in, 76
  Greece, in, 76
  Italy, in, 76
  JSB (England)
    less serious injuries, 75–76
    severe injuries, 75
  Netherlands, in, 77
  PIAB (Ireland), 73–74
  Spain, in, 77
legal information
  jury awards, 10–12
  reported cases, 11–12
  settled actions, 12
  unreported cases, 12
liquidate damages, 6
Luxembourg
  bespoke assessment system plus *barème*, 27

"Mac–JSB", 51–52
McEwan & Paton
  citation of, 15
  data comparison using, 13, 15
  introduction of, 13
  organisation of contents, 15
  source of assessments, as, 13
  status of, 13, 15

medical information
  haphazard nature of, 36–38, 49
  pre-action protocol on exchange of, 37
medical reports, 37
medicalisation, 57–59
multi-track hybrid tariff-based model, 57

Netherlands
  bespoke assessment system, 25
  leg injuries, awards for, 77
non-pecuniary damages
  categories of, 7
  generally, 6–7
Norway
  state control of assessment, 27–28

Pain and Suffering Damages Commission(er), 52–54
Pan-European Organisation of Personal Injury Lawyers
  assessment systems, research on, 24
  European *barème*, opposition to proposed, 46
partial tariff, 59–60
parties to case
  assessors of damages, as, 10
Pearson Commission, 40–41
Personal Injuries Assessment Board (PIAB) (Eire)
  adapting scheme for Scotland, 55–56
  background, 21–22
  cost of claims, on, 42
  leg injuries, awards for, 73–74
  medical reports, acceptance of, 37
  operation of, 22–23
  valuation of claims *see* **Book of Quantum**
personal injury
  death as, 5–6
  definition, 5
PIAB *see* **Personal Injuries Assessment Board**
popular opinion on level of damages
  Law Commission study, 53, 91–92
Portugal
  bespoke assessment system, 25
"precedent" approach to quantum, 14–15
preliminary issues, 1–5

quantification
  meaning of, 7–8

quantum
  authorities on, presentation of, 14–15
  meaning of, 7
  "precedent" approach to, 14–15
  time of assessment, 8–9

Ravaranni **tables**, 27
reform proposals
  JSB model
    departing from, 51–52
    using, 50–51
  multi-track hybrid model, 57–62
  need for, 49–50
  Pain and Suffering Damages Commission(er), 52–54
  PIAB model, adapting, 55–56
Reparation Law Reports
  "Quantum" notes in, 12
reported cases, sources of assessments, as, 11–12
restitution, 29
Rothley Group on the European Scale, 45
"rule of thumb" approach in jury awards, 10–11

schedule of damages, 14
Schmerzensgeld, 7
Scotland
  see also **Gill Report**; **Gill Review**
  bespoke assessment system, 25
  compensatory status of awards, 29–30
  judicial assessment in, 13–17
  Judicial Studies Committee, 51
  medical information, sources of, 37
Scottish Courts website
  JSB guidelines, use of, on, 17
  source of assessments, as, 13
Scottish Law Commission
  fatal claims, assessment of, 6
  quantification, on, 8
  role of, 2–3
  tariff for fatal cases, on, 30–31
settled court actions
  source of assessments, as, 12, 49
solatium
  definition, 7
Spain
  bespoke assessment system plus *barème*, 27
  leg injuries, awards for, 77

state control of assessment, 27–28
Sweden
  state control of assessment, 28

table and points system *see barème system*
tariff
  see also **Criminal Injuries Compensation Authority**
  absence of, 38–40
  CICA scheme as, 38
  fatal cases, in (proposed), 30–31
  human rights and, 32–34
  partial tariff, 59–60
  popular opinion on
    Law Commission study, 53, 91–92
  proposed new
    administration and, 60–62
    generally, 59–60
Tillburg Group *see* **European Group on Tort Law**
transparency of system, 34–38

Twelve Tables (Roman law)
  penalties, on, 5
typical cases
  assessment of injury
    Scots law, in, 77–83
  court-disputed non-pecuniary damages (medium value) (JSB use) (other disputed issues), 69–72
  court-disputed non-pecuniary loss (low value), 63–69

United Kingdom Judicial Studies Council, 51
unliquidated damages, 6–7
unreported cases
  JSB guidelines, use in, 17
  sources of assessments, as, 12

whiplash claims
  extent of, 46–47
wrongful death
  damages payable on, 5–6